Supernatural
LIVING

BOOKS BY LARRY KREIDER

Building Your Personal House of Prayer

Discovering the Basic Truths of Christianity

and

Building Your Life on the Basic Truths of Christianity

AVAILABLE FROM DESTINY IMAGE PUBLISHERS

Supernatural
LIVING

WISDOM, KNOWLEDGE, FAITH, HEALING,
MIRACLES, PROPHECY, DISCERNMENT,
TONGUES, and INTERPRETATION

LARRY KREIDER and DENNIS DE GRASSE

DESTINY IMAGE® PUBLISHERS, INC.

P.O. Box 310, Shippensburg, PA 17257-0310

*"Speaking to the Purposes of God for this Generation
and for the Generations to Come."*

This book and all other Destiny Image, Revival Press, Mercy Place, Fresh Bread, Destiny Image Fiction, and Treasure House books are available at Christian bookstores and distributors worldwide.

For a U.S. bookstore nearest you, call 1-800-722-6774.

For more information on foreign distributors, call 717-532-3040.

Or reach us on the Internet: www.destinyimage.com

ISBN 10: 0-7684-2837-8   ISBN 13: 978-0-7684-2837-7

For Worldwide Distribution, Printed in the U.S.A.

1 2 3 4 5 6 7 8 9 10 11 / 13 12 11 10 09

Dedication

This book is dedicated to our Lord Jesus Christ, the Giver of all gifts, and to the thousands of believers in Christ we have been privileged to minister to and with over more than 30 years of ministry.

Acknowledgments

We really enjoyed writing this book together. We could not have done it without Karen Ruiz, our editor and writing assistant from Partnership Publications. Thank you, Karen, for sharing your expertise with us. Great job! Thanks also to Peter Bunton, Katrina Brechbill, Michael Bailey, Wes Clemmer, David Miller, David and Nodya Havice, Shirley Graham and Nick Honerkamp for their valuable input. And a special thanks to Don Milam, Dean Drawbaugh, Don Nori Jr. and the entire Destiny Image team. You have been wonderful to work with. And finally, we are so grateful to the Lord for our amazing wives, LaVerne Kreider and Jeanne De Grasse, our partners in life and ministry.

Table of Contents

Introduction 11

Part I   **Why We Need the Supernatural Gifts** 13
Chapter 1   Gifts Are to Use! 15
Chapter 2   How to Be Filled with the Holy Spirit 27
Chapter 3   Jesus Ministers Through You. 37

Part II   **The Nine Supernatural Gifts** 49
Chapter 4   Message of Wisdom 51
Chapter 5   Message of Knowledge 57
Chapter 6   Faith 67
Chapter 7   Gifts of Healing 75
Chapter 8   Miraculous Powers (Miracles) 83
Chapter 9   Prophecy. 91
Chapter 10 Distinguishing Between Spirits 103
Chapter 11 Different Kinds of Tongues. 109
Chapter 12 Interpretation of Tongues 117

Part III   **Using Your Supernatural Gifts** 123
Chapter 13 Actively Waiting for God 125
Chapter 14 Tune In to God's Frequency 137
Chapter 15 Release What You Have 145
Chapter 16 Be Led by the Spirit 151
Chapter 17 Break Through the "Saran Wrap" of Fear 159
Chapter 18 A Time to Pray and a Time to Say 165
Chapter 19 Discriminating Between Soul and Spirit 171
Chapter 20 Things We Have Witnessed 179
Chapter 21 God Wants to Use You 185

Appendix 193

Introduction

For more than 30 years, we have witnessed and experienced firsthand average, ordinary believers ministering in the nine supernatural gifts of the Holy Spirit. And yet, for many, ministering in these supernatural gifts has either been controversial or appeared to be for only certain evangelists or seasoned spiritual leaders. We are totally convinced that God desires for all Christians to experience the supernatural gifts of the Spirit flowing through their lives so they can minister effectively to others. So we decided to write this book and include both our personal stories and the experiences of dozens of others throughout the world whom we know personally who have experienced effective ministry in a supernaturally natural way. This book is filled with sound biblical instruction with lots of practical insights that you can begin to immediately apply to your life. Since we are both common, ordinary men, we know that if God can use us, He can use anybody! Expect our God to use you in new ways as you experience His supernatural gifts flowing through you in supernaturally natural ways.

—Larry Kreider

To know and experience God is an amazing experience! It has been a blessing to walk with the Holy Spirit through nearly forty years of life and ministry. It has also been a great joy and satisfaction to see normal, everyday people moving in the power of the Holy Spirit. This book is the realization of a dream that is over two decades in coming. I believe that we have been called to role-model a walk in the Holy Spirit that is without hype or pretense. We have shared personal things in this book that were often costly to learn. Our prayer is that we could be like those who blazed the trail for others to follow. It is our hope that the following generations of believers will discover these truths and go further than we have ever been able to go. God bless you as you step up to the challenge of revealing Jesus to a lost and dying world.

—Dennis De Grasse

Part I

Why We Need the Supernatural Gifts

Chapter I

Gifts Are to Use!

A man and his wife arrived at their hotel on a three-day trip to Switzerland. After checking in late in the afternoon, they decided to eat in the hotel dining room, even though it was expensive and they were on a budget. The evening dinner was excellent, and when they asked the waiter to add the cost to their hotel bill, he nodded consent, smiling in a knowing way. To save money, the couple ate most meals out, but never had as fine food as that first evening. Receiving their hotel bill at the end of their stay, they noticed they had not been charged for that fine dinner. They learned, to their chagrin, that payment of advance reservations had included not only room but meals as well. They could have eaten every meal for all three days in the hotel dining room at no extra cost. How like many Christians! Unaware of what wealth the Holy Spirit has given us in the form of *spiritual gifts*, we go through life without using our resources.[1]

This book is about uncovering and using the nine supernatural gifts the Holy Spirit has given us. They will equip us for God's service, but we have to make use of a gift before it becomes functional! How many of us have received a gift that languished on a shelf because we had no motivation to use it? Over the years, we (Larry and Dennis) have been given various tools as gifts. Since neither of us are very handy when it comes to fixing things, just having the tools does not get the job done. Tools must be used to become helpful.

Our gifts have always been more with words: reading, writing, and public speaking. We both love to play guitar and sing songs. In fact both of us have composed a number of songs over the years that seemed to bless people. They would applaud when we were finished singing. Maybe they were just glad it was over! The point is that God has blessed every individual with gifts that are to be used as tools to do their God-appointed work.

Everyone's gifts are different. Some have many gifts, others have a few, but everyone needs to understand what their gifts are and ask God how to use them. We believe that many go through life not utilizing their gifts which remain as unused tools—unknown and untapped within their lives. Imagine a construction worker trying to build a house without the tools provided for him, or a secretary trying to type a letter without using the computer in front of her. God gives the gifts of the Holy Spirit so they can be the very resources at our fingertips to serve Him more fully. God is a gift-giver. He freely gives. To begin with, He gave us the unsurpassable gift of Jesus Christ. God giving gifts to unworthy people is a major theme of the Bible.

Gifts, Gifts, Gifts!

The Scriptures are filled with spiritual gifts that God wants to give us. Although the topic of this book is "the gifts of the Holy Spirit," it is helpful to take a bird's eye view of the many diverse gifts God generously gives. We could group these spiritual gifts into three categories:

Gifts of the Father—*inner motivational gifts for every individual* (see Rom. 12:3-8)

Gifts of Christ—*spiritual leadership gifts for individual leaders to train God's people to minister* (see Eph. 4:9-16)

Gifts of the Holy Spirit—*operational gifts to help all believers become ministers* (see 1 Cor. 12:7-11)

We notice that God gives inner motivational gifts to individuals that carry the very imprint of God the Father in that individual's life. The gifts of Christ are the gifts Jesus gave to the Church as special ministry gifts to individual leaders to "train God's people to do the work of the ministry." And finally, the gifts we focus on in this book, the gifts of the Holy Spirit, which help believers to "do the work of ministry."

Motivational gifts: We believe God, the Father, gives everyone on the face of this earth inner motivational gifts that carry a thumbprint that they have been created in God's image. These gifts are not dependent on our relationship with Jesus but are given to both believers and non-believers alike. Each gift is a special talent for a particular type of activity given to all persons. These gifts shape our personality types and provide our inner motivation.

Gifts of leadership: Another kind of gift God, the Son, gives is the five leadership gifts—apostle, prophet, evangelist, pastor, and teacher. These are gifts that have a specific purpose and function to encourage believers and train them to minister to others. These gifts are given to some people, but not to everyone.

Gifts of the Holy Spirit: Finally, there are the nine supernatural gifts of the Holy Spirit, the topic of this book. With these gifts, the Holy Spirit manifests Himself through us so we can help others. As with all the gifts God gives, they cannot be earned—they are freely given by God to His children. The gifts of the Spirit are an evidence that you have made Jesus the Lord of your life and have been filled with the Holy Spirit. There are different kinds of gifts because God works in different ways through each one of us for the common benefit of others in the church.

> *Now to each one the manifestation of the Spirit is given for the common good. To one there is given through the Spirit the message of wisdom, to another the message of knowledge by means of the same Spirit, to another faith by the same Spirit, to another gifts of healing by that one Spirit, to another miraculous powers, to another prophecy, to another distinguishing between spirits, to another speaking in different kinds of tongues, and to still another the interpretation of tongues. All these are the work of one and the same Spirit, and He gives them to each one, just as He determines* (1 Corinthians 12:7-11 NIV).

Notice that the Holy Spirit decides which gift(s) a person should have. But how do we know for sure which gifts we have? Sometimes we need someone to point them out to us or teach us how to use them. That's why we are connected in the Body of Christ—to help each other so we can use our gifts for the benefit of others.

One time, the Lord gave a supernatural message of special knowledge for a particular young man at a local church when I (Dennis) was praying for him. I asked if he played the violin. His response was a swift, "No." He almost seemed to be offended at the idea that he might play the violin. I did not blame him. I found the violin to be a vicious instrument. I tried to learn to play one once. It turned on me and caused my whole family to ridicule me and to howl in laughter each time I tried to play it. No sweet tones would come from that beast. It sounded like two cats screeching in the middle of the night. Well, back to the story. This young man had not even thought of playing one. He would admit to no desires in that direction at all. I simply told him that he could play one if he so desired.

Two years later I found myself back in that same church, only to find this young man playing the violin in the worship band. He had decided to take God at His word and had taken up the instrument. He was voted the most improved student of the year in the school orchestra during his first year. The next year he was moved to first chair in the school orchestra. He now played in church, and he had moved beyond just playing written music. He could play by ear as well. He was wonderful! He had a splendid talent resident within him that was previously unrecognized and unused. It just took someone to encourage him and plant a seed in his life.

Over the years, we have seen this phenomenon happen again and again—people, totally unaware of what was resident within their lives, just needing someone to point it out and to encourage them. Through these supernatural gifts, God has released many into their giftings and ministries. He has pointed out latent abilities and unknown talents and skills that he wanted released and activated. Many times people have come up to us and reminded us of a word of knowledge or encouragement that we had spoken into their lives many years before that we had forgotten about, that set them on a clear course for their life.

God enjoys seeing His kids perform. Both of us (Dennis and Larry) have children who are quite gifted in the musical realm. They play instruments and sing. They compose their own music and can perform it with grace. They have followed the Holy Spirit and have been used by the Lord to bring blessing to many. We cannot tell you how enjoyable and humbling it is to watch our children exercise their gifts and talents. We are sure that God feels that same joy when He watches us releasing His creativity and power through our lives.

Both Godly and Gifted

Before we go on much further, we want to clarify that the gifts of the Spirit are not to be confused with the fruit of the Spirit. Gifts are given to be used, but fruit must be grown. If we were to give you an appliance or a tool for a birthday gift, it would be free. It is a gift! All you need to do is to use it. But fruit starts out like a seed, and it must be cultivated and fertilized and watered in order to grow. The supernatural gifts of the Spirit found in First Corinthians 12 are gifts given to you to use to magnify God and help other people. The fruit of the Spirit found in Galatians 5:22-23—love, joy, peace, patience, kindness, goodness, faithfulness, gentleness, and self-control (all God's character)—comes as a seed in you and must be matured over time. Bible teacher Joyce Meyer once said, "God told me if I'd put half as much time in developing the fruit of the Spirit as I did in the gifts, I'd already have both. Gifts will get you somewhere but won't give you enough character to keep you there once you get there!" Your gifts will not be as effective as they should be unless the fruit of the Spirit is cultivated alongside it. It is from the character (the fruit) of Christ that your gifts will come forth in power.

Matthew 7:20 says it best, "Yes, just as you can identify a tree by its fruit, so you can identify people by their actions." We must always ask ourselves, "Are our actions displaying the fruit of the Spirit?" Possessing gifts does not indicate godly character. We must be both godly and gifted. Paul positioned the love chapter, First Corinthians 13, in the center of this section of Scripture that deals with spiritual gifts (see Cor. 12-14). As Christians, our love walk must be developed, first and foremost. Paul wrote that our gifts would amount to nothing if we did not have love. Love must be the governing principle in all spiritual gifts.

Be Available so the Gifts Can Operate

The gifts of the Spirit are not given privately for us simply to "experience." They are meant to be "exhibited" and "used." Paul told the Corinthian church that they must co-labor with God in manifesting spiritual gifts: "Since you are eager to have spiritual gifts, try to excel in gifts that build up the church" (1 Cor. 14:12 NIV). Paul counseled the Corinthians to try to excel in the gifts because, as Christians, we have a part in their operation.

 The gifts of the Spirit are not given privately for us simply to "experience." They are meant to be "exhibited" and "used."

As the Holy Spirit guides your life, you will see the gifts of the Spirit operate through you. Your job is to make yourself available so that the gifts can be exhibited. Did you ever wonder how many have received words of encouragement only to talk themselves out of it? How many seeds are lying dormant in our lives? How many have had desires for these things, only to be talked out of it by someone else?

When God speaks to us, whether through prophecy, the Bible, or just an idea or a dream, we must mix faith with what we hear. We could spell faith "R-I-S-K." If we want to experience God, we are going to have to be risk-takers. For some, the idea of being wrong is so traumatic they are unwilling to try anything. What a shame and what a waste. There are worse things than being wrong.

What Do You Dream About?

How does God let us know what he wants from our lives, and how do we discover these gifts and abilities that are hidden within us? When the young fiddler heard the word, "You can play if you want too," something obviously began to stir in his heart. What do you think about when you are quiet? Do you ever dream of doing something you have never done before? Philippians 2:13 says, "For God is working in you, giving you the desire and the power to do what pleases Him." These desires may come as a result of a seed planted by another, a seed planted while reading the Bible, or they may come by the inner working of the Spirit of God in your life. God will often send a confirming word to you. Once again, we must mix faith with what we hear. Your own mind may, often as not, fight with you and try to talk you out of pursuing this dream. It may be risky or dangerous to your self-preserving ways. Do you have desires and dreams that just will not go away? It could be a part of the picture.

Be a Participator Rather Than a Spectator

Paul told the believers at Corinth to pay attention to the gifts of the Spirit: "Now, dear brothers and sisters, regarding your question about the special abilities the Spirit gives us. I don't want you to misunderstand this" (1 Cor. 12:1). We cannot afford to ignore or be ignorant of these important gifts, because we desperately need them in order to function effectively for Christ. Another time, Paul encourages the church to "eagerly desire spiritual gifts" (see 1 Cor. 14:1 NIV). God made sure that they were recorded in His Word for our benefit. They are not just an interesting historical fact, but are available for us today. Keep in mind, these gifts are not for our benefit alone, but to benefit those in need of their power.

We have both gone through seasons where we have "pestered" God for them. We just had to have these supernatural gifts operating in our lives. We simply would not take "no" for an answer. We were totally convinced that these spiritual gifts were for today and that God wanted us to experience them.

 These gifts are not for our benefit alone, but to benefit those in need of their power.

We challenge you today to test this. Ask the Holy Spirit to reveal the truth to you. Begin to study the Scriptures and see what He will show you. He will open your heart and give you His understanding. It is the Holy Spirit who will lead you into all truth. He is the one who takes the things of Christ and brings them into your world. Since Jesus lives in you, He is able to be in you everything that you are not. He lives His life through you as you yield to His control. The Holy Spirit does not want you to be a spectator. Instead, He wants you to allow God to work through you. Who knows what precious gift may lie hidden in your life? Who knows what the Lord will do through you? The Holy Spirit is willing to share it with you today.

We will share many examples throughout this book of times we have seen the gifts of the Holy Spirit in operation. For example, I (Dennis) found myself in a large church in South Carolina. As we were worshiping the Lord I heard the Holy Spirit whisper His intentions of healing some people that morning. He elaborated that I would not have to touch them, but was to just speak out the words of knowledge and that He would heal them by His presence in the room. When I got up to minister I shared that word with the people and then spoke out several different words of knowledge. One was for people with ear damage. After I had spoken, I then gave people the opportunity to testify. Many shared their healings, and much rejoicing followed. I then said that if anyone else noticed anything they could wave at me and I would let them share their story. About five minutes later a man began to wave and shared that he was hearing out of an ear that had not worked for twenty-five years. His eardrum had been ruptured, and he consequently was deaf in that ear, but now was hearing perfectly. Another man shared that his ears were working better, too. He had experienced severe nerve damage in the war, but was now hearing sounds that he had been unable to hear before.

Being filled with the Holy Spirit is a prerequisite to releasing the power of God into your life. Jesus came to earth, became a man, and was able to perform miracles, healings, resurrections, and deliver words of prophecy. How was He able to do these miraculous works? The answer reveals to us the secret that God intends for us to walk in as well, if we're to experience victory in the Christian life: Jesus was the Man that He was because the Holy Spirit came upon Him and gave Him power to live a life that was pleasing to the Father.

Lester Sumrall, who founded the LeSEA network that reaches millions of people daily with the good news of Christ, once said, "When our Lord Jesus came to this earth to conquer it and redeem it, He functioned only within the framework of the gifts of the Spirit. His total ministry on earth was not as God, but as a man, functioning in the gifts of the Spirit. All the "miracles" Jesus performed were the result of a gift of the Spirit functioning at that time...The ministry Jesus performed on this earth was directed, guided, and energized by the Holy Spirit—the same Holy Spirit that you and I have today. We can expect to do the same works Jesus did if we will follow, line upon line and precept upon precept, everything the Word of God teaches. Each one of us has a right to every gift of the Holy Spirit without exception. Each believer in Christ has the right to any and every gift of the Spirit. When we leave ourselves out, it is through unbelief. We say, 'That is for someone else. It can't be for me.' But the gifts are for you! They are provided for the total Body of Christ, and you as a believer are a part of His Body."[2]

Do you know for sure that you are filled with the Holy Spirit? Are the spiritual gifts becoming evident in your life? If you are not sure, in the next chapter we will explain how to be sure you have been filled with the Holy Spirit.

Endnotes

[1] Leslie B. Flynn, *Gifts of the Spirit* (Colorado Springs, CO: Cook Communications Ministries, 2004), 213.

[2] Lester Sumrall, *The Gifts and Ministries of the Holy Spirit* (New Kensington, PA: Whitaker House, 1982), 265-268.

Chapter 2

How to Be Filled with the Holy Spirit

*A*ll genuine believers have the Spirit of God dwelling in them. First Corinthians 3:16 says, "Don't you know that you yourselves are God's temple and that God's Spirit lives in you?" The Holy Spirit lives within each child of God. The divine person of the Holy Spirit comes to dwell in you when you give your life to Jesus and receive Him into your life. He cares about you and has the power to help you. However, this does not mean you have been *filled* with the Holy Spirit.

When you were convicted of your sin before you received Christ, the Holy Spirit was outside of you bringing conviction. When you received Jesus, the Holy Spirit then came *inside* to live within you. But there's more! The New Testament depicts *two* distinct yet complementary aspects of receiving the Holy Spirit. Let's compare the two experiences.

After the disciples' encounter with the Holy Spirit when Jesus breathed on them and told them to "receive the Holy Spirit," He made it clear that their experience was still incomplete (see John 20:22). In His final words to them before His ascension, He commanded them not to go out and preach immediately, but to go back to Jerusalem and wait there until they were baptized in the Holy Spirit and thus given the power they needed to be effective witnesses.

...Do not leave Jerusalem until the Father sends you the gift He promised, as I told you before. John baptized with water, but in just a few days you will be baptized with the Holy Spirit...But you will receive power when the Holy Spirit comes upon you. And you will be my witnesses, telling people about me everywhere—in Jerusalem, throughout Judea, in Samaria, and to the ends of the earth (Acts 1:4-5,8).

So the disciples prayed and waited. During the festival of Pentecost, 120 of His disciples were gathered together in one place, and it happened!

On the day of Pentecost all the believers were meeting together in one place. Suddenly, there was a sound from heaven like the roaring of a mighty windstorm, and it filled the house where they were sitting. Then, what looked like flames or tongues of fire appeared and settled on each of them. And everyone present was filled with the Holy Spirit and began speaking in other languages, as the Holy Spirit gave them this ability (see Acts 2:1-4).

They had received the life of the Holy Spirit only a few weeks before when Jesus breathed on them (John 20:22), but this time they were *filled* with the Holy Spirit. They received a new dimension of the Holy Spirit's power.

This distinction between receiving the Holy Spirit at rebirth and being *filled* with the Holy Spirit is significant. Being *filled* is the Lord's provision for releasing the power of the Holy Spirit into the believer's life.

A Power Encounter

Saul was a devout Jew who was playing havoc with the Christians in the book of Acts. He was on his way to Damascus to persecute the early Christians when the Lord met him and did something supernatural in his life.

"Who are you, lord?" Saul asked. And the voice replied, "I am Jesus, the One you are persecuting! Now get up and go into the city, and you will be told what you must do." ...So Ananias went and found Saul. He laid his hands on him and said, "Brother Saul, the Lord Jesus, who appeared to you on the road, has sent me so that you might regain your sight and be filled with the Holy Spirit;" (Acts 9:5-6,17).

> Ananias called Saul "brother" because Saul was now a Christian. However, Saul still wasn't filled with the Holy Spirit. Many people say that when you're saved, you are also automatically filled with the Spirit. Although it is possible to receive and be filled with the Holy Spirit at conversion, it is not always so. Saul, who became Paul, was baptized in the Holy Spirit three days after he received Christ into his life. It happened when Ananias laid his hands on Saul and prayed.

The difference between receiving the Holy Spirit at salvation and being filled with the Holy Spirit can be explained like this: You can be led to a pool of water and drink from it (receive the Holy Spirit at salvation), or you can jump fully into the water (be filled with the Holy Spirit). It's the same water (Holy Spirit) but you have a completely different experience.

During the late 1800s, evangelist Dwight L. Moody was preaching and saw the same two ladies sitting in the front row night after night. Nearly every night, they came up to him after his meetings and said, "Mr. Moody, you need power." At first he resisted their remarks. However, months later, as he walked down a street in New York City, he had an experience with God and was filled with the Holy Spirit.[1]

The results were amazing! He preached the same sermons, but instead of two or three people giving their lives to Christ at his services, hundreds and thousands came to know Jesus. In his lifetime, more than a million people were kept out of hell because of the power of God on his life. What made the difference? He had been filled with the Holy Spirit and had received power.

 To enter into the fullness of what God has planned for our lives, we have no greater need than to be plugged into the power source.

The story is told of a Christian man who lived in a poor village in the interior of his nation who had the opportunity to come to a big city. Having never experienced the use of electricity before, he was fascinated when he saw electric light bulbs for the first time. He asked his host if he could have one to take back to his home. When he got back to his village, he hung the light bulb on a string in his hut. He was frustrated because it wouldn't work, until a missionary explained to him that it must be plugged into a power source. That's the way it is with us. To enter into the fullness of what God has planned for our lives, we have no greater need than to be plugged into the power source. Being filled with the Spirit is the gateway into a new dimension of the Spirit's presence and power in our lives, empowering us for ministry.

We Receive by Faith

Just like salvation comes by faith, so being filled with the Holy Spirit comes by faith. Faith is always a prerequisite for receiving.

Galatians 3:14 tells us explicitly "...we who are believers...receive the promised Holy Spirit through faith."

Not everyone's experience will be the same. We can pray and receive the Holy Spirit on our own or have someone pray for us to receive the power of the Spirit. Some believers have a dynamic, emotional experience at the time of their being filled with the Holy Spirit. They may begin to sing a new song that God gave to them in an unknown language or speak in tongues. Others simply take God at His Word and experience the reality of being filled with the Holy Spirit as a process over the days and weeks that follow.

The type of experience that we have is not of primary importance; the key is that we know by faith in the Word of God that we've been filled with the Holy Spirit. We need to *know* we are filled with the Spirit just as we need to *know* we have been born again.

It is possible to be baptized in water and in the Holy Spirit at the same time. Or, some may be filled with the Holy Spirit before they are water-baptized. It happened in Acts 10. Peter was preaching the gospel to the Gentiles in Cornelius's home when an amazing phenomenon occurred.

Even as Peter was saying these things, the Holy Spirit fell upon all who were listening to the message. The Jewish believers who came with Peter were amazed that the gift of the Holy Spirit had been poured out on the Gentiles, too. For they heard them speaking in tongues and praising God (Acts 10:44-46).

The people at Cornelius' house received the Word and were saved. The Lord immediately poured out the Holy Spirit on them in power, thus paralleling the disciples' experience at Pentecost. Being filled with the Holy Spirit brings a personal boldness and power of the Spirit in our lives.

A Personal Story

It was seven years after I received Jesus Christ as my Lord that I (Larry) was filled with the Holy Spirit. I could have been filled sooner, but I was ignorant of the Holy Spirit's work. Although I loved the Lord and was part of a youth ministry, I realized there was something missing in my life. I needed the power of the Holy Spirit. I sometimes attended Christian ministries where people were set free from drugs or other life-controlling problems, and I realized these people had a spiritual power that I didn't have.

After studying the Scriptures and being convinced this experience was based on the Word of God, I went out into the woods one day and prayed, "God, I want You to baptize me in the Holy Spirit." I prayed, but nothing happened. In retrospect, I can see that I had pride in my heart. I wanted to be filled with the Holy Spirit alone, on my own terms. I didn't really want anything too radical to happen! So, I humbled myself and went to a pastor who laid his hands on me and prayed for me. That night I was filled with the Holy Spirit.

After I was filled with the Holy Spirit, my life immediately took on a whole new dimension of power. It wasn't me; it was God. Being filled with the Holy Spirit gave me an intense desire to please Him. Before I was filled with the Holy Spirit, I was involved in a ministry where a few people had given their lives to the Lord. However, after I was filled, everything seemed to change. Hundreds of young people gave their lives to Christ during the next few years. I knew that it certainly wasn't anything that I was doing in my own power and strength. It was the Holy Spirit's power.

Although it took me several years from the time I was saved to the time I was baptized in the Holy Spirit, I believe it is God's will that we are born again and immediately receive the infilling of the Holy Spirit and the power of God in our lives. Acts 2 says that being filled with the Holy Spirit was not just for those at Pentecost, but for all who would believe in Christ throughout this age:

...you will receive the gift of the Holy Spirit. This promise is to you, and to your children, and even to the Gentiles—all who have been called by the Lord our God (Acts 2:38-39).

Receiving God's Good Gift

Some might ask, "Do I really have to be filled with the Holy Spirit?"

Our question right back would be, "Why would you *not* want to be filled?" The Holy Spirit is God's gift to you. But whether or not you receive and open that gift is up to you. Suppose you are given a gift of a tool you really needed. Before it can be effective, you must take the tool out and use it. The same principle applies to the Spirit of God. We need to receive the gift of the Holy Spirit by faith, and then begin to use all the wonderful individual supernatural spiritual gifts that accompany it.

Being filled with the Holy Spirit increases the effectiveness of a Christian's witness because of a strengthening relationship with the Father, Son, and Holy Spirit that comes from being filled with the Spirit. The Holy Spirit makes the personal presence of Jesus more real to us, and it results in wanting to love and obey Him more.

The early disciples made being filled with the Holy Spirit a requirement for anyone who was to be set apart for special responsibilities in the Church. "And so, brothers, select seven men who are well respected and are full of the Spirit and wisdom. We will give them this responsibility" (Acts 6:3).

God has already initiated His part in our receiving Christ and being filled with the Holy Spirit. It's up to us to receive by faith what He has freely offered. To be filled with the Holy Spirit is a personal act of faith, a decision that we make. Our heavenly Father wants to give us the gift of the Holy Spirit. "So if you sinful people know how to give good gifts to your children, how much more will your heavenly Father give the Holy Spirit to those who ask Him" (Luke 11:13).

Have you been filled with the Holy Spirit? If you are not sure, ask! Your heavenly Father wants you to receive the Holy Spirit, and He offers the infilling of the Holy Spirit to you freely![2]

Continue to Be Filled with the Spirit

We must reach out and receive the promise of the Spirit by faith. By faith we receive, and then are continually filled, day by day. When D.L. Moody was asked why he said he needed to be filled continually with the Holy Spirit, he replied, "Because I leak!"[3]

The early believers knew this, too, according to Acts 4:31: "After this prayer, the meeting place shook, and they were all filled with the Holy Spirit. Then they preached the Word of God with boldness." Many of these believers were already filled with the Holy Spirit at Pentecost in Acts chapter 2, but they needed to be filled again. We, too, must experience constant renewal.

Being filled with the Holy Spirit happens in the context of committed discipleship to Jesus Christ. Our hearts must be right with God so He can pour out His Spirit on us. As we live in obedience to Christ, there will be a greater awareness and presence of the Holy Spirit in our lives. We will deepen our relationship with the Father and grow in our love for others.

 As we live in obedience to Christ, there will be a greater awareness and presence of the Holy Spirit in our lives.

God wants to use you to see change come into people's lives. But it takes the Holy Spirit's power to "break through." The Lord wants to use you to touch others' lives for eternity. People in your family will be changed when you are filled with the Holy Spirit. It may not happen immediately, but it will happen! It won't be through your natural ability, but by Christ who is at work in you through the Holy Spirit.

Endnotes

[1] *Dwight L. Moody Directory*, 1837-1899, http://www.kamglobal. org/BiographicalSketches/dwightlmoody.html; accessed September 17, 2008.

[2] A booklet entitled *How can I be filled with the Holy Spirit?* by Larry Kreider is available through House to House Publications at www.h2hp.com.

[3] Joel Comiskey, "The Filling of the Holy Spirit," http://www.cbn.com/spirituallife/BibleStudyAndTheology/ Discipleship/Comiskey_SpiritFilling.aspx; accessed January 21, 2009.

Chapter 3

Jesus Ministers Through You

*I*n a Russian Orthodox Church in Moscow the members greet each other by embracing and looking into each other's eyes and saying, "In your eyes I see the face of Christ." We can locate Jesus most meaningfully as we look into the eyes of our fellow Christians.

One day, a group of strangers came up to the disciples and expressed a desire that has been felt by people down through the ages. Speaking to Philip they asked for the privilege to see Jesus: "Sir, we wish to see Jesus." They wanted to meet Him face to face. When their request was relayed to Jesus, instead of going to them physically, Jesus answered them by saying,

> *Now the time has come for the Son of Man to enter into His glory. I tell you the truth, unless a kernel of wheat is planted in the soil and dies, it remains alone. But its death will produce many new kernels—a plentiful harvest of new lives* (John 12:23-24).

It seems clear from how Jesus responded that to know Him and what He stood for did not necessarily require seeing Him or being physically with Him. In fact, Jesus clearly is speaking of His death when He said (our paraphrase), "If I die, like a grain of wheat, I will reproduce Myself many times over." The thought is plainly there for all to see—Jesus' death and subsequent resurrection created the possibility of God's residence within every Christian as He multiplied Himself many times over. He sent the Holy Spirit to dwell inside each of us, and that's how we can see Jesus—in each other. As we allow Jesus to walk and talk and live His life through us, Jesus is revealed to the world.

We Experience Christ in Each Other

In the following chapters of this book, we will build the case that Jesus is alive and well in His Church. Think about it for a moment. Jesus knew that, while on this earth, He was limited by His singularity—He could only be in one place at the time. You could go to where He was and see Him, receive ministry from Him and get to know Him, but that would have been an arduous task involving travel, time and expenses. At best, many had to worship Him from afar. Only a privileged few had the opportunity to fellowship with Him as confidants.

Today Jesus is in His Church, which literally involves millions of Christians around the world. This provides myriad opportunities for people to have encounters with Christ. Are we saying that we have taken the place of Jesus? Yes and no. No one can take Jesus' place, but He now lives in us, as believers. He is seated in the heavens, but is present in His Church on the earth. Let's consider a few verses in the Bible that confirm these thoughts. Here, Paul, the apostle, reveals the great mystery of the ages.

> *This message was kept secret for centuries and generations past, but now it has been revealed to God's people. For God wanted them to know that the riches and glory of Christ are for you Gentiles, too. And this is the secret: **Christ lives in you**. This gives you assurance of sharing His glory* (Colossians 1:26-27).

Angels longed to look into this mystery. Humankind has always had a hunger for the knowledge of eternity. Thankfully God is not the invention of man. We are His creation and His plan has always been to have a family. Because of Jesus we are able to be part of that family. The plan is simple: Jesus lives in us by the Holy Spirit; His presence and the continuing work of His grace transforms us into sons of God. The words "in you" express the thought of *in us* and *among us.*

 Jesus lives in us by the Holy Spirit; His presence and the continuing work of His grace transforms us into sons of God.

The Church is the Body of Christ on the earth. Jesus is no longer limited by His physical body. He fills us with His Spirit and has chosen to continue His ministry through us. For this purpose, the Holy Spirit, the promise of the Father, has been sent to earth to fulfill this mission: fill the people of God with the Spirit of God in order to reveal the Son of God. Jesus will return to earth in His glorified body, but we believe that before He does He will glorify Himself through His Body, the Church.

> He existed before anything else, and He holds all creation together. Christ is also the head of the church, which is His body. He is the beginning, supreme over all who rise from the dead. So He is first in everything (Colossians 1:17-18).

Compelling Evidence

We may wonder why we do not see more evidence of Christ's presence in the church than we do. That is a good question. We believe one of the key issues is that of headship. Who is the actual head of the Church? Who is it that controls what takes place in the Church? In many instances we have structured things so tightly and with such control that there is no room for Jesus. Man decides what is allowable, what is for today and what God will or will not do in our generation. In many cases we have talked ourselves out of much of God's will for the Church. One brother in Christ expressed it this way: "We say 'that was for the Jews,' 'that is for the future,' and 'God doesn't do that any more.'"

While visiting a friend's church, I (Dennis) listened to my friend teach an adult Sunday school class from First Corinthians. He had just finished with chapter 11 and I was curious as to what he would teach from chapter 12, which explains the nine super-natural gifts of the Spirit. To my surprise, he skipped right over chapter 12 and went to chapter 13, the love chapter. After the class I asked him what happened to chapter 12. His response was, "That is not for today." I later challenged him and eventually led him and his family into a deeper understanding of what the Holy Spirit could do today. He was filled with the Holy Spirit and began to personally experience the supernatural gifts of the Holy Spirit; his faith was no longer just an intellectual exercise—it was now experiential.

If we are going to experience Christ in His Church, we may have to adjust our theology. One of the reasons we experience lit-tle may be that we expect little. One of the problems we face is that of skepticism. In America, it is as if a cloud of skepticism and intel-lectualism covers the land. We often see through the eyes of our own experiences or lack of them. We may have even been influ-enced by other skeptics, or we could use the word "unbelievers," who have no use for spiritual certainties. They seem to be experts in explaining away the miracles of the Bible, using convincing arguments to persuade us that the Scriptures are not relevant today. The Bible becomes a guidebook filled with nice ideas, none of which we can live up to or experience.

The story is told of a shoe manufacturing company that sent two salesmen to the outback of Australia to try to stimulate some business. After several weeks one salesman wired back to the company and said, "Business here is lousy. The natives don't wear shoes." The following day the second salesman sent his update saying, "Business here is great. The natives don't wear shoes." Two salesmen had two very different outlooks on the same scenario. Could it be that our view of God and His ways has a lot to do with whether we are participants who see opportunities through the eyes of faith or just spectators when it comes to supernatural spiritual gifts?

We Need the Gifts Today More Than Ever Before!

Many people have an indifferent attitude about these wonderful gifts. Some people do not believe they are for today. They believe the gifts of the Spirit were for the early Church and not for today's Christian. They claim the early Christians *needed* God's supernatural power for the overwhelming task they faced as a fledgling movement, and when they no longer needed the gifts to illuminate and magnify the proclamation of the gospel, the gifts ceased. This belief that all miracles and gifts of the Spirit ended with the death of the apostles is called *cessationism.* Jack Deere, in his book *Surprised by the Power of the Spirit,* says, "This belief is not based on Scripture itself but is an attempt to explain the absence of the power of the Spirit in the Church. Augustine, in his early life, was a cessationist, but he completely reversed his position because of the number and frequency of miracles he witnessed in the fourth century church."[1]

Down through the ages of church history, there are many records of people exercising spiritual gifts:

Dr. Philip Schaff, the well-known church historian, wrote, "The speaking with tongues, however, was not confined to the Day of Pentecost. We find traces of it still in the second and third centuries."

Irenaeus (A.D. 115-202) was a pupil of Polycarp, who was a disciple of the apostle John. He wrote, "In like manner do we also hear many brethren in the church who possess prophetic gifts and who through the Spirit speak all kinds of languages, and bring mysteries of God, whom also the apostles term spiritual."

In Souer's *History of the Christian Church*, the following statement is found: "Dr. Martin Luther was a prophet, evangelist, speaker in tongues and interpreter, in one person, endowed with all the gifts of the Holy Spirit."

Rev. Boyd was an intimate friend of the famous evangelist, Dwight L. Moody. He wrote about Moody, "When I got to the rooms of the Young Men's Christian Association [Victoria Hall, London], I found the meeting on fire. The young men were speaking with tongues, prophesying. What on earth did it mean? Only that Moody had been addressing them that afternoon![2]

Although during certain times in Church history they may have been rare, the gifts never ceased. If the supernatural gifts of the Spirit were not highly visible in the Church throughout the ages, it was not because God removed them from the scene or believers no longer needed them. Their rarity simply represented failure on the part of God's people to believe the Scriptures with simple faith.

Believers often reclaim the New Testament dynamics of experiencing the supernatural gifts of the Holy Spirit during times of renewal in Church history. This brings new life to the Church. It is at these times that believers again take John 14:12 to heart: "…anyone who believes in me will do the same works I have done, and even greater works, because I am going to be with the Father." We believe today's Church is once again hungry for His supernatural power in order to live victoriously. We need the gifts today more than ever before because we need His power!

Paul, the apostle, told the Church to exercise spiritual gifts while it waits for the return of the Lord Jesus. And He has not come back yet!

> *…so that you come short in no gift, eagerly waiting for the revelation of our Lord Jesus Christ, who will also confirm you to the end, that you may be blameless in the day of our Lord Jesus Christ* (1 Corinthians 1:7-8 NKJV).

Faith to Live!

We are both rather simplistic. We believe the only book fit to translate and explain the Bible is the Bible itself. We are not interested in theories of man that explain away the truth of Scripture. It is amazing how many so-called experts treat the Bible as just a history book. They tell us that all of these things happened in the past, but cannot happen now! Some even seem to doubt the reality of the history, as if the stories portrayed in the Bible are not real, and treat them as though they are mere allegories and myths. We have even heard it said that the Bible contains the truth, but you have to sort it out from the allegories and fairy tales.

This book is being written on the premise that the Bible is the Word of God and is the truth. We build our case on the authority of the Bible. We will also share experiences that accompany such an outlook. We are convinced that the truth taught in the Bible is not just for our intellectual exercise, but is to be experienced as well. It is not just a faith to believe, but a faith to live.

Most of us have never been to Heaven, but we believe Heaven is real. Most of us have never seen God, but we believe He is real. We believe that Jesus died and rose again for us because the Bible tells us so. Our faith is built upon the revelation of the Holy Scriptures. When we put our faith into action, we experience the reality of the person of Jesus Christ. He is a lot more than an idea, or a historical figure; He is real and alive today. We can know God, the Father, if we will get to know the Son:

> *Jesus told him, "I am the Way, the Truth, and the Life. No one can come to the Father except through Me. If you had really known Me, you would know who My Father is. From now on, you do know Him and have seen Him!" Philip said, "Lord, show us the Father, and we will be satisfied." Jesus replied, "Have I been with you all this time, Philip, and yet you still don't know who I am? Anyone who has seen Me has seen the Father! So why are you asking Me to show Him to you? Don't you believe that I am in the Father and the Father is in Me? The words I speak are not My own, but My Father who lives in Me does His work through Me. Just believe that I am in the Father and the Father is in Me. Or at least believe because of the work you have seen Me do. I tell you the truth, anyone who believes in Me will do the same works I have done, and even greater works, because I am going to be with the Father. You can ask for anything in My Name, and I will do it, so that the Son can bring glory to the Father"* (John 14:6-13).

Jesus came to reveal the Father to us. We have found that faith will take us places our intellect sometimes doesn't want to go. God can do and does things that are unexplainable by anyone. We have witnessed tumors disappear, scoliosis being healed, cataracts melt off eyes, new ear drums created, frozen joints released, cancer gone, new joints created in a moment of time, and many more miracles. These things are not intellectual exercises, but are the results of experiential faith in Jesus Christ. They are a result of Jesus exercising His headship. They are a result of hearing and obeying the Holy Spirit. We hope that you will be stirred in your faith as you read this book. Allow the Holy Spirit to reveal Christ to you and then to reveal Christ through you.

We Must Respond to Faith

Many times while ministering at churches and conferences throughout our nation and in the nations, we are asked this question: "As you travel around the Church, what do you see happening?" The answer is not always so easy to find, but we believe we have an answer. We perceive that the Church is currently in a waiting mode. We are like the lame man lying by the pool, waiting for God to stir the waters. We wish someone would put us into the waters when they are stirred. We long for a move of God in our lifetimes. We want God to do something! God has already done something. He has given us eternal life. He has given us the Holy Spirit and has anointed us to have power to minister to others. We firmly believe that Jesus has longings in His heart, too. We believe He longs for His Church to awaken. He wants His people to know who they really are in Christ. In many ways, the Church is like a paraplegic, the head is alive and full of ideas and plans, but the body is unresponsive.

 Faith will take us places our intellect sometimes doesn't want to go.

When we were born into the Kingdom of God, we received a vision from the Lord. We saw something in our spirits that has never gone away and has never relinquished its hold upon our hearts. We saw the Church marvelously alive. We saw the Body of Christ functioning in the grace gifts of the Holy Spirit. We understood that the gifts of the Holy Spirit were for all and they were for now. Over the years we have experienced God in many wonderful ways and we have seen him minister to many through these powerful and relevant gifts. We have watched the gift of faith awaken the Church and enable believers to move in mighty signs and wonders. We have seen the people of God take hold of the presence of God and move into the supernatural arena where anything is possible. We wish to share with you the simplicity of ministering with Jesus and seeing Him move in your life as you simply hear and obey. You can witness miracles and signs and wonders too. This is not the heritage of a few, but the legacy Jesus has left for His entire Church, His Body in the earth today!

In the next nine chapters we will look at each of the supernatural gifts of the Holy Spirit found in First Corinthians 12:7-11: a message of wisdom, a message of knowledge, faith, gifts of healing, miraculous powers, prophecy, distinguishing between spirits, different kinds of tongues, and interpretation of tongues. We will list them in chronological order as they appear in Scripture, but often Bible teachers classify the nine gifts into the following three groups:

"Discernment" or "revelation" gifts: a message of wisdom, a message of knowledge, and distinguishing between spirits (the power to know)

"Demonstration" or "power" gifts: faith, gifts of healing, miraculous powers (the power to do)

"Declaration" or "vocal" gifts: different kinds of tongues, interpretation of tongues, and prophecy (the power to say)

Although each of these nine spiritual gifts in these three categories are unique, in many ways, they are often interconnected like the links on a chain. Each gift is linked together with others in such a way that when you pull one, you are pulling the entire chain. Sometimes it is difficult to divide the links and distinguish between them because they are so interrelated. Let's begin in the next chapter by looking at the first gift, the message of wisdom.

Endnotes

[1] David Ireland, *Activating the Gifts of the Holy Spirit* (New Kensington, PA: Whitaker House, 1997), 31.

[2] Lester Sumrall, *The Gifts and Ministries of the Holy Spirit* (New Kensington, PA: Whitaker House, 1982), 265-268.

Part II

The Nine Supernatural Gifts

Chapter 4

Message of Wisdom

*To one there is given through the Spirit the
message of wisdom* (1 Corinthians 12:8 NIV).

*P*eter understood net fishing. He had years of experience in
the family business. But after a long night on the lake
without catching a single fish, he was ready for a change, so he
allowed Jesus to use his boat to teach a crowd of listeners on the
shore (see Luke 5). Jesus stood in his boat teaching and after He
finished, He told Peter to cast his net on the other side of the boat.
It sounded pretty crazy to Peter; after all, Jesus had no experience
as a fisherman, because He was trained as a carpenter. But Peter did
as Jesus suggested and caught so many fish the boats began to sink.
How did Jesus know where to cast the nets? He had received a message of wisdom from His heavenly Father!

A Message of Wisdom Is Given to Help People

God wants to help people and is willing to give us information
to assist us to that end. This "power to know" gift involves speaking the hidden things—unknown things we would not naturally
know about someone or something. It is a fragment of God's wisdom, received supernaturally and delivered naturally. This gift
operates through the Holy Spirit and in the realm of faith, as it

provides insight regarding people, places, and things. A message of wisdom often comes to us as a strong impression. God will not tell us everything about another person's life or circumstances, but He will share those things that will help them.

Our own knowledge and wisdom are not enough; we need supernatural help.

Many of us have people who come to us with various needs in their lives. We soon discover that our own knowledge and wisdom are not enough; we need supernatural help. In fact, sometimes people seeking help have no clue as to what is wrong in their lives. As Spirit-filled Christians, we must make it a practice to not only listen to people, but to listen to the voice of the Holy Spirit as well. He will whisper insights into our heart. We can begin to minister out of those insights and see the Lord uncover the real problems.

He will whisper insights into our heart.

One time I (Dennis) was asked to help with a particular couple at a church where the pastor was a friend of mine. I listened and prayed for the couple as they shared their problems with me. Suddenly the Holy Spirit revealed something to me and I began to speak to them about what I was seeing and hearing. They looked at each other and then at the pastor. Apparently the Holy Spirit had hit a vein of truth and had uncovered the real problem. It was not what they had thought, but the Holy Spirit had revealed to them the real issue they were facing. We should mention here that the Lord holds us accountable for this "insider information" that

He is giving to us. We cannot use it for our own ends. The Lord expects us to have Christ-like character and hold in confidence those personal things that are revealed.

We have both experienced the gift of a message of wisdom in operation in our lives many times. The Holy Spirit is more than willing to partner with us for the sake of serving His people, both the saved and pre-Christians, those who are in the process of coming to Christ. Many times, as we have served as visiting ministers in churches, the Lord has given us a supernatural message of wisdom to help a pastor or another believer that is not based on anything we have learned naturally.

A few years ago, I (Larry) had the privilege of investing some money into a business that paid great dividends. I was ready to reinvest the money into the same company again, but my wife LaVerne encouraged me not to do it. She had no natural wisdom or financial savvy as to why we shouldn't reinvest; she just had a strong impression that it was not the right thing to do. I have learned to listen to what the Lord speaks to my wife, so I did not invest. We later discovered that the company was involved in massive financial difficulties, and had I invested money into it, I would have lost every cent I put in. I am so grateful I followed the input that came from the gift of wisdom my wife received that made no sense to me naturally, but it was the word of the Lord. The Lord used this gift in operation in LaVerne's life to protect us from financial hardship.

If we only rely upon our training and experience, we may be missing some important information. If we only lean on what someone else's perceptions are we will only be imparting what we know with our natural minds. Natural knowledge is fine, up to a point. But we want to see and know things that God sees and knows. Do not be surprised if some are offended at this approach. We also have discovered that some who come to us for counsel are really not interested in anything but confirmation of what they want to do. They have already made up their minds about what they intend to do and have no room for adjustments in their thinking.

Biblical Examples

We see an example of a message of wisdom functioning for Paul in Acts 23. Paul was about to lose his life at the hands of an angry religious mob. The officials threw him in prison to keep him from being torn to pieces, and the Lord spoke to him by a message of wisdom, "Be encouraged, Paul. Just as you have been a witness to Me here in Jerusalem, you must preach the Good News in Rome as well" (Acts 23:11). Paul didn't know at that point that he would even see the light of day, much less go to Rome, but God revealed the future to him. That was a message of God's wisdom revealed to Paul.

Another time, when Paul first visited Corinth, he received great opposition and threats. In the natural, one would conclude that it was time to move on. But again, he received a supernatural word of wisdom by means of a vision that it would be safe to stay in Corinth (Acts 18:9-11).

Jesus assured His disciples that He would give them words of wisdom to say when they would be arrested for following Him. He said, "When you are arrested, don't worry about how to respond or what to say. God will give you the right words at the right time" (Matt. 10:19). Another time, Jesus directed His disciples to go to the next village, find a donkey and her colt and tell the owner that the Lord needs them, and bring them back to Jesus.

Most people would not allow you to take away their donkey and colt just because you said, "The Lord has need of them." Yes, this was divine, directive wisdom, and God had prepared the owners' hearts to receive it. We see that the results of this word of wisdom were to open hearts and meet a practical need.[1]

How Do We Respond to a Message of Wisdom?

God may not always give us His wisdom directly. Often as not, He will give it to someone else. It may be a spouse, our parents, our spiritual leaders or even someone we do not especially like or respect. It will then take humility and a love for the truth to allow us to receive it this way. It is a lot easier when it is just you and God, but when He involves others we can get a little stubborn about it.

One occurrence of the word of wisdom operating in my life was while I (Dennis) was pioneering a new church on the East Coast of the USA. As a church, we had been meeting in less than ideal circumstances. We felt that we wanted a more permanent location in the city and began to look around for something appropriate and affordable. We soon found a property that would meet our needs. It was a building that had been used as a warehouse. It had the right amount of space and some additional property. When we inquired about the property, the price needed to secure it was more than we had. It seemed as though it was not going to happen. We just didn't have enough money to complete the deal.

I began to pray about this situation and suddenly a thought came into my mind. Through the real estate agency, we offered to give them what we had as cash on hand with the understanding that we would then rent the building for a year. All of the rent would then go to the building and we would have the balance of the down payment at the end of the year. The real estate agency said that the owner would never go for that deal and would not even give him the proposition. Once again I felt the nudging of the

Holy Spirit. He seemed to tell me to call the owner myself. That is not the way it is usually done, but I called anyway. To make a long story short, the owner went for the deal and we purchased the building. Today it is a live and strong church that is a witness to the faithfulness and love of the Lord.

I must tell you that I am not a businessman, but the wisdom that came to me was from the Lord. There are times when we need to discern the right thing to do. God may lead us against conventional wisdom. We may find ourselves doing things that others may think will not work, but the Lord knows what to do and He will tell us if we will listen to Him.

It has been said that we have two ears and one mouth, signifying that we are to listen twice as much as we talk. That is good advice. We must learn to listen to the Holy Spirit. We must pray in the Spirit and wait upon the Lord to give us some insight. As this happens, we can move into the realm of the Holy Spirit. Keep in mind, one word from God can do more than a million words from us!

Endnote

[1] Derek Prince, *The Gifts of the Spirit* (Kensington, PA: Whitaker House, 2007), 60-61.

Chapter 5

Message of Knowledge

*...to another the **message of knowledge** by means
of the same Spirit* (1 Corinthians 12:8 NIV).

A friend of mine (Larry) had an acquaintance who was coming home late one night to his apartment in New York City. Suddenly a robber jumped out of the dark and told him to give him all of his money. With a gun pointed at him, the only thing that came to his mind was to trust God. God gave him an instant message of knowledge, and he began to tell the thief about his mother, who had prayed for his salvation and who constantly talked with him about his need for the Lord. The robber was frightened and said, "How did you know those things? I'm out of here! This is too crazy!" His friend was spared from being robbed and possibly harmed because he believed that the supernatural spiritual gifts are for all believers and practiced them.

A young man was struggling with depression and came to see me (Larry) for help. He told me that he had grown up in a Christian home, wandered away from God, and after years of drug and alcohol abuse he had an encounter with the Lord. Even though he had recently made a commitment to give his life to Christ, he was still struggling with a lack of peace in his life. We talked for some time, and then I suggested we spend time praying together. As soon as I closed my eyes and began to pray, I saw a clear mental picture of a liberty bell. It did not make sense to me but I asked him if a liberty bell meant anything to him. He said it made no sense to him at all. Then he suddenly remembered something. "Come to think of it," he said, "I have continued to drink alcohol in secret and have given the impression that I am free from an addiction to alcohol. There is a liberty bell on the bottle that I am now drinking." The Lord showed me a liberty bell by a supernatural gift of knowledge that I had no prior information about, to jolt his thinking about an area of secret sin in his life. God got his attention, and today, he is free from his addiction to alcohol.

A message of knowledge is supernaturally imparted by the Holy Spirit and is only a portion of God's total knowledge. This "power to know something we do not know in the natural" gift is not the gift of all knowledge, but the gift of a *word* of knowledge given by the Holy Spirit. God does not give us all of His knowledge, but just a word (part) occasionally. It is a portion of God's endless storehouse of knowledge. It can come as a thought, impression on our mind, or a vision.

> The word of knowledge is the supernatural exposure of the mind of God regarding something in the past or present. The fragment of information may relate to a person, place, thing, feeling, or idea. The operation of this gift, however, is neither an acute sensitivity to human behavior nor spiritual revelations based on already known facts about a person. It is verbally sharing a fragment of God's knowledge.[1]

The gifts of a message of wisdom and a message of knowledge are often tied together. A message of knowledge gives us facts, and a message of wisdom shows us what to do about those facts. You could say knowledge is the raw material and wisdom builds on it.

Message of Knowledge

  The gifts of a message of wisdom and a message of knowledge are often tied together.

Like a message of wisdom, a message of knowledge is not something we have learned or can reason out. It is supernatural insight or understanding of circumstances and situations. We are passing on to others information from the Holy Spirit that He wants them to know. We are like a mailman whose job is to deliver a message to the person whose name is on the envelope. It is not our message—it comes from God. The mailman doesn't have to know or understand the person who the letter is addressed to. His job is simply to deliver the message. We are the delivery person. When we do just as the Holy Spirit asks us—no more and no less—then the message of knowledge will be delivered to the right person in the right place at the right time.

  A message of knowledge is supernatural insight or understanding of circumstances and situations.

A message of knowledge releases faith in our hearts and the hearts of the recipients. God does not dangle blessings in front of our noses just to tease us. He wants to heal His people. He gives us supernatural knowledge to inspire faith and to help people receive their blessings from His hand. The "message of knowledge" has been a constant part of my (Dennis') life and ministry. I have seen myriads of healing because of this powerful gift. I have discovered that when the Lord tells us what He is going to do it takes very little faith to see it done. After all, we are just reporting what we are hearing or seeing. It is up to the Lord to actually do the work. Our work is to believe; His work is to perform His words.

On one occasion, a word of knowledge revealed a person with a film over his eyes. God expressed His willingness to heal if the person would respond to the word. An older gentleman came forward and declared that he had a cataract on one of his eyes. He also stated that he had just had an operation to remove one from the other eye and was scheduled for surgery in a few days' time. I (Dennis) asked him if he believed that God could heal him, and he affirmed his faith. I remember commanding the cataract to come off his eye in the name of Jesus. He returned to his seat and I continued to minister to others. After the meeting he approached me with a little ball of matter between thumb and forefinger. I asked him what it was and he stated that after returning to his seat his eye had begun to itch. As he rubbed it this substance, the cataract, came off in his hand. It had literally melted off his eye. The next night he testified that the eye that God had healed was better than the one that had been operated on.

On another occasion I was praying for a long line of believers who had come forward for healing at a meeting. One man was there with intense pain in his shoulder. He could not raise his hand above his shoulder. As I stood before him, praying softly, the Holy Spirit showed me exactly what to do. I spoke out what I saw in the Spirit, because I wanted the people to realize that healing was really not a hard thing to do. I instructed the man that when I touched his shoulder he was to immediately raise his hand as far as he could. I just touched his shoulder and his hand shot up fully over his head. He had been unable to raise his hand like that, but the word of knowledge had shown me a way to not only see him healed, but to demonstrate the simplicity of moving with the Holy Spirit.

The Word of Knowledge

Sometimes I get some thoughts in which the Holy Spirit describes an affliction, sickness, or disease. With the thought comes the understanding and the faith to reach out for healing. I sometimes actually experience some symptoms of the sickness myself. The first time this happened, I experienced a sharp pain in my lower back as I was leading worship. Not knowing what it was, I began to pray. It did not seem normal, as I had no back problems. I finally ventured out into the realm of risk-taking and voiced the symptom I was feeling. I felt that the Lord had revealed a problem, and He had the cure. My pastor's wife came to the altar for prayer and was healed on the way!

At times, I actually feel as though someone is tapping on different areas of my body when I receive a word of knowledge. As I identify the area, people respond and are healed. Sometimes in my imagination, I see the human body. As I look at the different areas of the body, certain things will stand out. I am aware of the eyes or the ears, for example. At that point, the Holy Spirit may speak and give me the particulars. If He does not, then I just speak out about the things I see. As I speak out those impressions, healing is released. Most of the time, I lay hands upon people for their healing, but sometimes the Lord tells me to simply speak out the words, and He does the work.

When you receive a message of knowledge for a person regarding healing and know the exact location of the pain or sickness without any natural means of knowing, it produces faith because people are hopeful that if God knows what the problem is, He can heal it. That is why a message of knowledge is often used as a tool to bring faith into operation for healing.

Biblical Examples

An example of the message of knowledge in the Old Testament occurs at a point in history when the king of Syria was warring against Israel. The invading king was convinced that he had a spy in his midst because every plan he made was conveyed to the king of Israel. Finally, he was told by one of his servants, "Elisha, the prophet in Israel, tells the king of Israel even the words you speak in the privacy of your bedroom!" (2 Kings 6:12).

Jesus spoke a message of knowledge to the Samaritan woman at the well (see John 4:15-19). As a stranger, He could not have known her history, but God revealed it to Him: "You don't have a husband—for you have had five husbands, and you aren't even married to the man you're living with now" (John 4:18). The supernatural disclosure of the woman's marital state of affairs resulted in her salvation.

In Acts 10, God gave Peter a supernatural word of knowledge in the form of a vision. He told Peter to go to a Gentile's house to bring him the gospel. This instruction went against Peter's background and training. But Peter listened to this word from God, and it paved the way for Cornelius and his family to receive the Holy Spirit. If Peter had gone to school all his life, he couldn't have learned such knowledge from natural means. The all-knowing God gave this knowledge to Peter and helped him to realize that all people were created equal in God's sight.

What if No One Responds?

There may be times when you receive an impression from the Lord and you share it with a person or a group of people and no one responds to it. We have both had this happen on several occasions. One time when I (Dennis) was ministering at a church I received a message of knowledge about someone suffering from a pancreatic condition. I released the word from God because it came very clearly to me. No one responded. I persisted as I went down the list. No one had a friend or relative or even an acquaintance with such a problem!

It looked as though I had missed God. I just could not get a release from this message impressed on my spirit, so I prayed and released my faith. Several months later, I heard that my own uncle, living in Maine, was healed from a serious pancreas condition about the same time that I had received that word. Was that just a good coincidence? I believe it was the mercy of God for my lost uncle.

Sometimes when I minister in a meeting, no one will respond to a message of knowledge until after the meeting is over. Many times I will try to get someone to respond to the message of knowledge but to no avail. After the meeting, however, someone will come for prayer. It will be exactly what I had spoken out.

We May Not See the Whole Picture

Have we ever missed God? We are sure we have. The Bible says that "...our knowledge is partial and incomplete, and even the gift of prophecy reveals only part of the whole picture!" (1 Cor. 13:9). As with any gift of the Spirit, sometimes we may not receive the complete word from the Lord but just a piece of it. God sometimes uses others to add to it to get the full picture.

God knows that we want to be a channel for His blessing to flow to others. We often explain to people that we receive impressions. We are simply giving expression to the impressions we are receiving. We may not always be describing their problem exactly, but if their problems are close to what we are describing, we encourage them to respond.

Messages of Knowledge Through Visions

Sometimes we receive messages of knowledge through visions the Lord gives to us. Visions can come in different forms. Some visions are like virtual reality. You are there. You hear the sounds; you smell the flowers. The visions that we usually have are just quick mental impressions or mental pictures.

There is one that stands out in my mind. During a quiet time, as I (Dennis) was leading a worship service, I saw a picture of an x-ray in my mind's eye. It looked like a hand. I prayed about it and decided I was willing to take a risk! I spoke out what I saw. A young man who had hurt his hand that very day responded. As I prayed for his hand, there was an instant healing.

Sometimes my visions show me what is happening. I remember asking someone with an ankle problem to respond. A young girl came forward. As she came, I saw a flash of God's power touch her ankle. I did not see this with my natural eyes, but with the eye of the spirit. I believe this is the place that we call imagination. I was not imagining it happening, but the Holy Spirit used that faculty to communicate to me and to allow me to see what was taking place in the realm of the Spirit of God. As I looked at her face, it was filled with wonder. I told her that I had just seen the power of God touch her ankle and that she was already healed. She confirmed what I had just witnessed. Often I see those kinds of things with my spiritual vision. Imagination is a God-created faculty.

These supernatural spiritual gifts are sometimes given to us during public Christian meetings and church services, but they have also been given to us to minister to people in everyday life. A friend of mine (Larry) was on a crosscountry flight when he saw a vision of the word "Adultery" written across the chest of a passenger sitting next to him. He struck up a conversation with the man and mentioned to him that the Lord had showed him he was involved in an adulterous relationship. The man was so shocked that he repented and gave his life to Christ before the plane touched the ground. My friend was demonstrating the supernaturally natural way that God intends the gifts of the Spirit to work. Certainly, it took faith on the part of my friend to step out initially and speak God's words. And this takes us to the next gift of the Spirit—the gift of faith.

Endnote

[1] David Ireland, *Activating the Gifts of the Holy Spirit* (New Kensington, PA: Whitaker House, 1997), 128.

Chapter 6

Faith

*...to another **faith** by the same Spirit...*
(1 Corinthians 12:9 NIV).

We were driving to the Dallas/Fort Worth Airport in a big pick-up truck owned by a Texan businessman (everything in Texas is big!). He was telling me (Larry) that he and his wife had been childless for many years, and it was a great struggle for them. They had tried everything they knew to do, and the doctors gave them no hope of having a child. As he drove into the airline terminal a gift of faith rose up in my heart for this couple to conceive a child. As I opened the door and stepped out of his truck, I reached across the seat and grabbed his hand and spoke into his life that he and his wife would be conceiving a child in the near future.

It kind of scared me to hear myself saying this. I did not want to give them a false hope, but I really felt it was from the Lord. A year later I was back in the same church and the businessman and his wife walked up to me before the service began and showed me their new baby boy, Samuel, who was conceived within a month of my receiving this gift of faith. His pastor told me that when I spoke into his life at the airport the businessman felt a surge go through his body and he knew that the Lord had done something supernatural. I carry a picture of little Samuel with me in my Bible as a reminder that we serve a supernatural God who wants to continue to use us all to minister in a supernaturally natural way.

What Is the Supernatural Gift of Faith?

The "gift of faith" is the special ability that God gives to you to discern with extraordinary confidence and unwavering belief in God's ability to fulfill His purposes. The gift of faith is not your theology. It is not saving faith (see Eph. 2:8) or your confidence or hoping something will happen. It is not faith confessions, ordinary faith (see 2 Cor. 5:7), or the prayer of faith. The spiritual gift of faith is one of the demonstration, or "power to do," gifts. It is the supernatural manifestation of the Spirit of God that miraculously drops the assurance of the answer to your prayers into your heart, even before you see it happen with your natural eyes. It is believing that you have it when you pray (see Mark 11:24). It ceases to be faith the minute you see it come to pass. It was the gift of faith that caused Abraham to claim that God had given him a son even before he saw any natural evidence. He understood that God "calls things that are not as though they were" (see Rom. 4:17 NIV). Stephen, full of faith, was enabled to perform miracles (Acts 6:8).

It's rather amusing, but one time God gave me (Dennis) a gift of faith to trust Him to banish a fly from the house. Somehow one of those annoying, buzzing house flies had gotten into our house. This thing was not only loud, it was fast. Our home was laid out in a big circle. I could walk around from room to room and that fly was always ahead of me. He wouldn't land, but I could hear him. It sounded like an airplane flying around my house! I finally gave up on catching him and was in the process of leaving. As I walked out the door I heard the Holy Spirit whisper to me, "Why don't you command him to come out?"

Looking around to make sure no one was in earshot, I commanded, "Fly, I command you to come out in the name of Jesus Christ!" Immediately I heard that fly buzz by me and out and through the open door. I was amazed. Who would think that God cared about a house fly? The operation of the gift of faith caused my own faith to grow, helping me to understand a little more about the importance of obeying the Lord, even in little things like flies. I would consider these events as miracles. I have witnessed many of them over the years and have heard many other equally amazing stories.

A person with the gift of faith acts in complete confidence of God's ability to overcome obstacles. A gift of faith causes us to ask God for what is needed and trust the Lord for His provision. Often, the gift of faith and gifts of healing have strong ties that connect.

While pastoring in Delaware, there was a family that had recently joined our fellowship. I (Dennis) knew a little about their lives and some of their struggles but had never really ministered to them prophetically. I felt an inner urge from the Holy Spirit to do so on a Sunday morning. As I was ministering to them I heard myself speak to the husband in a commanding voice that God was healing his neck "right now." He had been in an accident over a decade earlier that left his neck with the vertebrates frozen together and wired together. He had not slept in bed an entire night for over fourteen years and lived in constant pain. He went home unchanged, and at bed time laid down. He shared the next day that when he awoke, he sat up and realized he no longer had any pain. His frozen neck was able to move around. In other words, he went to bed one way and got up another! That is the power of the word of the Lord when we are willing to mix it with faith. I will have to admit that the "word" took me by surprise.

When the gift of faith operates it changes everything. I know the difference between my faith and the gift of faith. I can tell the difference when I am moving in the faith of God—there is no room for doubt or unbelief. Anything is possible when this gift is operating. I have also discovered another important operation of the gift of faith. I often share testimonies of healings that I have observed over the years. As I have shared these stories I have noticed that the level of faith begins to rise in the hearts of those who are listening. I often share the message of the simplicity of walking in the Spirit. I feel that God has commissioned me to take the mystery out of the supernatural arena. I have watched the gift of faith ministering to individuals as I share the simple truths of the Bible, enabling them to take hold of these truths and to experience God in higher dimensions.

This faith does not come by study. It is not the faith that is a normal part of every Christian. For example, there is a natural faith we have that tells us that when we plant a seed it will produce a crop of some kind. Or if we go fishing in the right spot, we will catch fish. In fact, even non-Christians have this kind of faith.

The gift of faith is different from other types of faith. This faith is a gift given to those who need it in order to fulfill the will of God. This is the kind of faith that allowed Moses to part the Red Sea. This kind of faith makes us immovable and unshakeable. When we are moving in the gift of faith we are moving in the faith of God.

It is a special faith that supernaturally achieves what is impossible through human instruments. We observe the gift of faith in operation when God, through the power of the Holy Spirit, performs supernatural exploits that cannot be humanly explained. These exploits cannot be what is done ordinarily; otherwise, they would have no relation to the supernatural gifts of the Holy Spirit.[1]

The story of three Hebrew young men—Shadrach, Meshach, and Abednego—who refused to bow down and worship the golden image of Nebuchadnezzar, the king of Babylon, is an example of supernatural faith (see Dan. 3). They knew that God would take care of them. They were thrown into a fiery furnace that had been heated seven times hotter than usual and not a hair on their heads was singed.

 We observe the gift of faith in operation when God, through the power of the Holy Spirit, performs supernatural exploits that cannot be humanly explained.

George Muller, who by faith operated an orphanage in Bristol, England, often moved in the gift of faith during his life and ministry.

George Muller cared for 10,000 orphans over a period of sixty years, receiving $5 million in the process. He began the work with only two shillings in his pocket. Without once making known any need, he received enough to build five large homes, able to house 2,000 orphans, and to feed the children day by day, all by faith and prayer. Never did they go without a meal. Often the pantry was bare when the children sat down to eat, but help always arrived in the nick of time. One morning when not a speck of food or milk was on hand to feed the hundreds of hungry orphans seated expectantly at the breakfast table, Mr. Muller prayed, "Father, we thank Thee for the food Thou art going to give us."

There came a knock at the door. A baker stood there. "I was awakened at 2 A.M. and felt I should bake some bread for you." A few minutes later came another knock. A milkman said, "My milk wagon just broke down in front of your place. I must get rid of these cans of milk before I can take the wagon for repairs. Can you use this milk?" Muller testified that thousands of times they were without food for another meal and without funds, but not once did God fail to provide food.[2]

Biblical Examples of a Gift of Faith

Inspired by the gift of faith, Paul declared that Elymas, a sorcerer who opposed his preaching, would be temporarily struck blind (see Acts 13:11). It was as Paul said. When the proconsul saw what had happened, he became a believer because he was amazed that Paul, through the power of the Holy Spirit, performed a supernatural exploit that could not be humanly explained.

When Jesus calmed the storm (see Mark 4:35-41), He just spoke to it. This is an example of divine authority through a gift of faith. In Acts 9:39-41, when Peter raised Dorcas from the dead, he prayed and received the gift of faith as he told her to arise. She did!

The gift of faith was demonstrated through Paul in Acts chapter 16, when Paul and Silas were in prison. They had been beaten and placed in the inner dungeon with their feet clamped in the stocks. There was no way they could help themselves. But God gave them supernatural faith in their dire circumstances. The Bible says that they sang praises to God at midnight. There was an earthquake and all the prison doors flew open. God's supernatural faith released them!

Releasing Faith in Others

We have also experienced the Lord using us to release faith in others. We believe that this is also the gift of faith at work. Often the Lord will have us share some of the things that He has accomplished in others. We will share some testimonies of healings and miracles. We can literally sense the faith building in the people. It makes ministry much easier when the believers we are ministering to have received the gift of faith themselves.

While visiting a brother in Christ in the hospital, I (Dennis) spent some time reading the Scriptures to him and encouraging his faith. He had been diagnosed as having cancer of the throat, and his doctor came in to chat just before the surgery. He spent the next five minutes speaking fear and unbelief into this brother. I was very upset! After the doctor left the room this brother said, "It does not matter what he said, I believe the Lord."

God's word had released faith. He actually came through that surgery far better than the doctor had imagined. We can build faith in people's hearts as we allow the Lord to speak through us. It is "Christ in us, the hope of glory." (See Colossians 1:27 NIV.)

I can remember a time when the gift of faith was very instrumental in my life. I was home for a 30-day leave from a U.S. Army base in Germany. It was several days before my return, and I was broke—without a penny to my name! The Lord had instructed me to give away what little money I had.

The flight to Fort Dix, New Jersey, was leaving in two hours, and I still did not have the money. I should have been worried. I had to get to Germany, and I did not have one cent. Somehow I just knew that the needed money would come. My faith was unflappable! It was not hard to believe, even though it was only a short time before the departure to the airport. Within the two hours' time, someone gave me the money for my ticket. God is faithful! I can remember thinking, "This isn't just my own faith; this is the faith of God working in me!"

I have experienced that gift working in me many times since then. The Lord never fails. I want to make it clear that it was up to me to hang onto the faith that God had deposited into my spirit. I would be tempted to get nervous. I would look into my spirit and ask, "Is faith still there?" It would still be there, so I just hung onto it.

 The gift of faith, along with the gifts of healing and miraculous powers, are some-times called the "demonstration gifts" and they often work closely together.

It certainly helps if we can look upon these stretching times as adventures. Life is exciting when we are looking for the hand of God to move. We often wonder, "How is God going to do it this time?" We are never disappointed.

The gift of faith, along with the gifts of healing and miraculous powers, are sometimes called the "demonstration gifts" and they often work closely together. In the next chapter we will discuss another of the demonstration gifts—the supernatural gifts of healing.

Endnotes

[1] Lester Sumrall, *The Gifts and Ministries of the Holy Spirit* (New Kensington, PA: Whitaker House, 1982), 87.

[2] Leslie B. Flynn, *Gifts of the Spirit* (Colorado Springs, CO: Cook Communications Ministries, 2004), 157-158.

Chapter 7

Gifts of Healing

*...to another **gifts of healing** by that one Spirit*
(1 Corinthians 12:9 NIV).

The concerned mother and father looked down at their 18-month-old daughter. She was one in a long line of children that had either died as infants or been still-born. She had become ill and now lay dead before them. This time, though, they had reason for hope. They had recently become Spirit-filled believers and their faith was in action. They called upon the church to pray with them. Other Christians joined with them to pray for the child, and the results were amazing. Though the child had been gone for nearly two hours, the power of God revived her. She is still alive today; I (Dennis) know, because she is my mom, born in 1920.

God always gets the last word in any situation He chooses. Perhaps the doctor has told you that you only have a few days to live. That may be their determination, but God does not consult the medical profession to get their opinion. He does what He does best, the miraculous. I remember the story of another infant who was born with many problems. The doctor told the mother that he would not last for an hour. Amazingly he did, and they adjusted their timetable. They forecasted that he would not last through the night. When he did they then said that he would not live long enough to go home from the hospital. When he was taken home they said he would never live long enough to start school. I am reporting that this man who was also born in 1920 was my dad! He is still alive; in fact, he was still driving a big truck cross-country at the age of 85. Today he is 88 and still works over 30 hours a week. God is amazing! God had a plan for my parents, and He had a plan for me. In fact, if it were not for the resurrection of the dead, I would not be here. He intervened in our family line to insure that we had the opportunity to fulfill His plan for our lives.

Working with God in the Gifts of Healing

The "gifts of healing" are the virtue of Christ being released through a human agent. God longs to intervene in our lives. There are times when God will do something sovereign without human involvement, but most often we, or someone else, are a part of the miracle.

  The "gifts of healing" are the virtue of Christ being released through a human agent.

Jesus said He only did what He saw the Father doing. The Father is the great initiator. He was the one motivating Jesus to heal, raise the dead, and cleanse the lepers. When confronted by the Pharisees about the man healed at the pool, Jesus said that His Father was working and that He, Jesus, was working. This is the work of God, and He wants us to work with Him.

What Is the Difference Between Healings and Miracles?

The Bible makes a distinction between gifts of healing and miracles because they are different—a healing is usually progressive and a miracle is frequently instant. In his book *The Gifts of the Spirit,* Derek Prince makes this distinction:

> Essentially, a healing relieves the body of disease or injury. It is often imperceptible to the senses. It may also be gradual; it does not necessarily happen instantaneously or even in a very short period of time. On the other hand, a miracle is usually perceptible to the senses and almost instantaneous, and it produces a change that goes beyond healing.[1]

Although some healings may be instantaneous, most are more of a process. The source for both is from the Spirit of Christ. Over the years, I (Dennis) have witnessed the Lord heal too many things to list. Scoliosis of the spine has been healed several times. Joint diseases have vanished. People have had their sight restored. Cancer has been healed. Heart problems have vanished.

Notice that the "gifts of healing" are plural! There are different anointings, specialized ministries so to speak, that can work for us. Some people have an anointing to heal back problems and skeletal problems. Others may have a special anointing to heal scoliosis of the spine. There have been eyes healed, ears opened, burns healed, growths removed. The list goes on and on. Some people's healing is manifested almost instantly while others may take awhile to appear. We would have to say that we must press on in these areas. We cannot stop praying for people just because we do not see the results we want to see. The results are in the hands of the Lord. Our job is to pray. He takes care of the rest.

You may have a lot of faith and success praying for cancer, while someone else may see a lot of blind eyes opened. We have seen some who have received a healing begin to move in faith to see others healed of the same afflictions. First Corinthians 3:9 declares that we are God's fellow workers. In other words, God does not just do it all Himself, but gives us the opportunity to work with Him. He even provides the tools for the job. If we had to come up with the ability to heal, we would be in trouble. Thank God that we do not have to; God provides all that we need to succeed.

Obviously, we see people getting healed every day through medicine, exercise, a change in diet, and sometimes even a change in attitude. God has designed our bodies to respond in this way, but sometimes those things alone just do not work, and God is willing to intervene. Jesus did not seem to turn anyone away that came to Him for healing or deliverance. Probably no one has the same kind of results that Jesus had, but we are convinced that the more we minister to the sick, the more healings we will see. The supernatural healing power was associated with the ministry of Peter so that even his shadow brought healing (see Acts 5:15-16). Thank God that He is the same, yesterday, today, and forever!

While traveling in Antigua, Guatemala, I (Dennis) received an emergency call from a dear friend and mentor. The doctor had just discovered cancer in his body. It was a particularly serious kind of cancer that was spreading quickly through his body. The cancer had already spread to one of his kidneys and on his adrenal gland. They expected it to go quickly to his lungs. The news had a sobering effect upon me and I began to pray for him. I was leaving for home the next day and as I flew toward the United States, I was praying in the Spirit for my dear brother in Christ. The Holy Spirit spoke to me and said, "This is not a sickness unto death, but I will do a work in him and his family through this." I was so excited that I called him from the phone in the airplane and I shared the word with him. He had a rough time of it, but he did survive and became totally cancer-free. He went back to see the doctor who had discovered the cancer, and the doctor acted as though he was seeing a ghost. He could not believe that my friend was still alive. Needless to say, the doctor received an ear-full about the grace, mercy, and power of God from my friend. The gift of faith combined with the gift of healing allowed me to see beyond the gloom of the doctor's prognosis. It allowed me to see from God's point of view. I had no doubt of the outcome. God had said it and He would do it.

A Time to Pray and Say

You have to learn how to release yourself in faith for healing. There is a time to pray and a time to say! If we want to see God move, we need to get beyond the praying stage and move into the saying stage. Jesus did not ask God to heal the man beside the pool, instead He commanded him to get up and take his bed with him. Peter did not pray for the lame man at the entrance of the Temple, instead he commanded him to rise up and walk. Peter even gave him a hand getting onto his feet.

One night a group of us were meeting in our home. It was the core group of a church that I was pioneering in West Palm Beach, Florida. We had been worshiping and had stopped to take some prayer needs. One young sister in Christ shared how she had been having some difficulties. The doctor had examined her and declared her need for surgery. This surgery would make it impossible for her to have any more children, but needed to be done. I remember the faith that came up in my heart in that moment. I asked her if she would like us to pray for her. Her response was, "Go ahead, but I don't think that it will do any good." My faith was not deterred and I remember declaring healing for her body. She returned the next week, after seeing the doctor again. He did not understand what had happened. Apparently she had a lot of scar tissue in her female organs that necessitated their removal. As he examined her one last time before the surgery he could find no scars. He told her, "Go home and have children." She did; in fact she had three of them.

A lady in a church in Stone Mountain, Georgia, had been in an auto accident and her back was severely injured. She shared that she was going to be traveling to Florida and was concerned about being able to endure the trip. When I prayed for her, the Lord put her on the floor and began to "operate" as her whole body began to tremble under the reality of God's presence. She later said she had made the journey without a problem. God had undertaken for her and healed her.

We must always remember that there are many ways to be healed. The greatest way to be healed is to pray for yourself. More people are healed by praying for themselves than all the other ways combined.

The second way is to have a family member pray for you. Millions of healings have been the result of mothers and fathers praying for their children. If families would develop their practice of this truth, they would not stop with their own families, but would reach out in prayer to their entire neighborhoods.

Another way to be healed is to call the pastor(s) and elders of your church. This biblical way is shown in James 5:14-15:

Are any of you sick? You should call for the elders of the church to come and pray over you, anointing you with oil in the name of the Lord. Such a prayer offered in faith will heal the sick, and the Lord will make you well. And if you have committed any sins, you will be forgiven.

You are to call for the spiritual leaders in your church who are full of faith and full of the Word. As they lay hands on you and anoint you with oil, you will be healed.

My (Larry's) mother-in-law was given six months to live by her doctor due to a mass found in her pancreas. He told us it was inoperable. She asked the elders of her church to pray for her according to James 5, and she felt heat go through her body as they prayed. This happened over 12 years ago. She is now 93 years of age! Jesus is our healer.

Then there are those who have a specialized gift of healing. Through this ministry the Lord gives certain individuals special gifts to pray for specific diseases.

We can experience these powerful gifts by allowing ourselves to be used by God in any way He may choose. We should not put limitations on what God can do with us. God, who can raise the dead, can use us any way He pleases! Are you ready for some radical Christianity? If you are, you will not find it in the safety zones of your faith; you will need to become a risk-taker. Have you ever seen people jump out of helicopters and snowboard down some distant mountain peak? They risk life and limb to do some stunt that is only important to them and their ego. When we become risk-takers for God, it is for His glory. The things that He does can only be done by Him to lift up the name of His Son. That is why we take risks. God is looking for some volunteers for a "mission impossible." May we give Him your name?

Are you ready for some radical Christianity? If you are, you will not find it in the safety zones of your faith.

Now let's talk about the gift of miracles. Bear in mind, how a person is healed—whether it is through the working of miracles, the gifts of healing, or the gift of faith—is really not the issue. The important thing is that he is healed! This always brings glory to God.

Endnote

[1] Derek Prince, *The Gifts of the Spirit* (Kensington, PA: Whitaker House, 2007), 128.

Chapter 8

Miraculous Powers (Miracles)

*...to another **miraculous powers***
(1 Corinthians 12:10 NIV).

The atmosphere had a strange feel to it. I (Dennis) commented to my wife, Jeanne, that there were going to be tornadoes somewhere in the area. If you have ever been around them, you know what I mean. I prayed for protection for our home and my family as well as the surrounding property and equipment. I even spoke in faith to the heavens and declared the protection of God over us all. We were renting a home from a Christian family that farmed for a living. That evening as we sat in the family room of our home, I heard what sounded like a freight train go over our house. Suddenly it was over, but the television was snowy with no picture. We had an outside antenna that was on a tall tower beside the house; the antenna used a motor to turn it in order to get a signal. My first thought was that the wind had turned the antenna away from the right direction. I used the control to turn it back with no success. It was dark outside the house, but after turning on the back door light I could see the tower was lying flat on the ground.

The next morning I looked in the back yard to see the damage. The tower was made of heavy metal, but was bent over just above the ground. The cornfield was about thirty feet away from the back door and I could see a patch of corn that had been pushed flat. It looked as though someone had placed a large plate on it; it was a perfect circle about fifteen or twenty feet across. Then I noticed the old grain elevator that stood nearby was missing. When I went out the front door I saw another circle in the corn near the front of the house. I could picture what had happened in my mind. That tornado had touched down just down the road from our house, had bounced over the roof, taking the tower as it went. It then touched down behind our house and cleared our neighbor's house and carried that old grain elevator down to the next road, which was about a quarter mile away.

 The gift of miraculous powers is a "demonstration gift" and is similar to the gift of healing.

You might think that was just a coincidence. I believe it was a miracle. I believe that God heard my declarations. I have made it a practice to declare the things that are in my spirit. It might not always be God, but it sure doesn't hurt. You may think this is crazy, but if it is just let me enjoy it!

The gift of miraculous powers is a "demonstration gift" and is similar to the gift of healing. The results are dramatic. Several years ago, while in England, I prayed for a woman who had burned her arm. Her arm was wrapped in a bandage from her elbow to her wrist. When we prayed, I felt nothing, but then it was not *my* miracle. Sometimes I can feel the anointing (being aware of His presence with me) touching people as I pray for them. Other times I feel absolutely nothing. I have come to realize that it does not matter what I feel. What is important is to release whatever faith I have and to move in obedience with the Lord.

Her husband later wrote and told me the details of the accident and how God healed her. She had been taking a roast out of the oven when she spilled hot grease all over her arm. The doctor said she would be scarred for life. She had blisters half as big as apples all over her arm. Her husband wrote, "We got up the next morning after you prayed, and the bandage was soaking wet. We removed the bandage, and the skin came off with it. There was brand new skin underneath—no blisters, no scars, no pain!" Now that is a miracle!

Miraculous Defined

We're all familiar with expressions like, "the miracle of modern medicine," or "the miracle of science," or "the miracle of childbirth." Nevertheless, when the Bible talks of miracles it is referring to something that cannot be explained by science or medicine. A miracle is something that enters our experience and contradicts the natural ways in which something takes place.

The New Dictionary of Theology states, "The word *miracle* comes from the Latin *miraculum,* meaning 'a wonder.' It suggests supernatural interference with nature or the course of events."[1] When God uses us to bring about a supernatural intervention in the natural order of things, He is giving us the "gift of miraculous powers." God cuts through to intervene, and we experience a miracle. The Greek word for miracle is *dunamis* which means "power and might that multiplies itself."[2] The gift of miracles operates closely with the gifts of faith and healings to bring authority over satan, sickness, and sin.

The writer, Leslie Flynn, defines miracles well:

A miracle is God stepping into His universe, setting aside the ordinary laws of nature to do something extraordinary. The owner of a complicated model railroad usually operated it from a control box, but on rare occasions he stepped amidst the miniature tracks to pick up by hand an engine or box car to reposition it. Our Creator set laws in motion by which He operates the world, but on occasion, when it serves His purpose, He has intervened to overrule some natural law. An answer to prayer, though unusual, would not qualify as a miracle unless the processes of nature were short-circuited.

The miracles of Jesus and the apostles evidenced:
power over disease (which relates more to the gift of healing),
power over demons,
power over nature (stilling storm, walking on water),
power over matter (water into wine, loaves and fishes),
power over death.

When Peter raised Dorcas from the dead, "it was known throughout all Joppa; and many believed in the Lord" (Acts 9:42 KJV). After Paul's miracle of pronouncing blindness on the sorcerer Elymas, "the deputy…believed, being astonished at the doctrine of the Lord" (Act 13:12 KJV).[3]

Miracles and Faith

Jesus performed many specific miracles in His three years of ministry on earth. His first miracle was turning water into wine (see John 2:1-3). Another miracle was when Jesus fed five thousand people by multiplying five loaves of bread and two small fish (see Matt. 14:17). With many miracles found in Scripture, an act of faith brought them into being. Jesus put clay in a blind man's eyes (see John 9:6), and He spit and touched a deaf man's tongue (see Mark 7:33). He once told a man to go wash in a specific pool of water. When he performed this act of faith, he was healed!

In the Old Testament, the prophet Elijah took his coat and struck the water of the Jordan River. It parted so he and Elisha could walk through on dry ground (see 2 Kings 2:8). When they reached the other side, the river again ran normally. Elijah activated his faith by using his coat, and a miracle took place.

Miracles and Deliverance

In Scripture we discover a relationship between miracles and the casting out of demonic spirits:

John said to Jesus, "Teacher, we saw someone using Your Name to cast out demons, but we told him to stop because he wasn't in our group." "Don't stop him!" Jesus said. "No one who performs a miracle in My Name will soon be able to speak evil of Me" (Mark 9:38-39).

Here, Jesus was referring to the casting out of demons as doing a miracle. Another example of the connection between miracles and deliverance from demons is found in Acts 19:11-12. "God gave Paul the power to perform unusual ("special" in the KJV) miracles. When handkerchiefs or aprons that had merely touched his skin were placed on sick people, they were healed of their diseases, and evil spirits were expelled."

The word "unusual" or "special" tells us miracles were normal in the early church, but that here was something even outside the norm. In Scripture passages where an actual miracle or miracles is specified, therefore, there is generally a reference to evil spirits going out. This is one of the manifest demonstrations of the power of God.[4]

As I travel to many nations, I (Larry) have seen demonized people set free through the miraculous power of God again and again. The name of Jesus and the blood of Jesus have great power and authority against the enemy. In Latin America, North America, and Africa, I have seen people writhing on the floor like snakes as demons spoke through them, but time and again, I have experienced the miraculous power of God releasing them from demonic bondage. When they desired freedom and believers broke the power of the enemy over their lives through the name of Jesus, they were set free. Every time I have experienced this, I witnessed a miracle.

Miracles Manifest Christ's Presence

"What do you want Jesus to do for you?" I (Dennis) often ask people. I get them to express what they are requesting a miracle for, and then I can agree with it. Recently a young man came to me requesting prayer for flat feet. I agreed with him in prayer and he told me that something was happening. About thirty minutes later he showed me the arches that God had created for him as a result of our prayers.

I know personally one well-known minister of the gospel who had a terrible speech impediment. When God called him to preach he could barely talk. He finally decided to trust Jesus to heal his tongue and was miraculously healed of his affliction. He became a wonderful speaker and has touched many lives with the truth of the gospel.

  The gift of miracles will always bring the ministry and message of Jesus Christ to the forefront.

It is wise to remember that Paul says in First Corinthians 12:7, "A spiritual gift is given to each of us so we can help each other." Miraculous powers, like any of the spiritual gifts, are given so we can help each other and show who God is. Some miracles take place instantly, while others take a season of time to manifest. It is important that when we are supporting others who are trusting God for a miracle, that we meet them at their point of faith, and that we do not in any way say or do anything that makes them feel guilty because the miracle has not yet happened. There are many variables when it comes to receiving miracles from our God. And we are all in the process of learning from Him. We should never desire the miraculous because they make us look good. What we should really want is that Christ be honored through our love for others as they are set free from sickness and oppression. The gift of miracles will always bring the ministry and message of Jesus Christ to the forefront with power. Miracles point to Jesus and give glory to His Name.

Endnotes

[1] David Ireland, *Activating the Gifts of the Holy Spirit* (New Kensington, PA: Whitaker House, 1997), 134.

[2] W.E. Vine, *Vine's Expository Dictionary of Old and New Testament Words* (Old Tappan, NJ: Fleming H. Revell Company, 1981).

[3] Leslie B. Flynn, *Gifts of the Spirit* (Colorado Springs, CO: Cook Communications Ministries, 2004), 181-182.

[4] Derek Prince, *The Gifts of the Spirit* (Kensington, PA: Whitaker House, 2007), 144-145.

Chapter 9

Prophecy

*...to another **prophecy*** (1 Corinthians 12:10 NIV).

While sitting with a small group of single people in our family room discussing the blessings and struggles of singleness, my wife LaVerne and I (Larry) soon realized that many in the group desired to be married. None, however, were in serious relationships. All of a sudden I felt a strong urge to give a message from the Lord to one of the girls sitting on the couch. I looked at her and said to her emphatically, "Your husband is on the way." I knew it was the Lord speaking through me prophetically. She then informed me that a friend she had met while serving in missions in Europe was on the plane from Amsterdam to America at that very moment. He was coming to see her to talk to her about a possible relationship. I had no clue this was happening. And guess what? About a year later they were married.

What Is Prophecy?

When the Lord speaks a message through one person for the benefit of another, it is called a "prophecy." When a prophetic word is given, it is for the purpose of knowing that God will speak directly to you. The Lord will reveal to you that the prophetic word given is a personal message from Heaven for you.

When a prophetic word is given, it is for the purpose of knowing that God will speak directly to you.

About those who prophesy, the Bible says, "…one who prophesies strengthens others, encourages them, and comforts them" (1 Cor. 14:3). In the Old Testament, prophecy was often given to bring judgment, but in the New Testament it is for strengthening, encouraging, and comforting believers. Sometimes prophecy is foretelling a future event while at other times it can be a message of encouragement for God's people.

Prophecy in the New Testament

The New Testament prophets revealed Jesus through their words of encouragement and insights on coming events, and it is the model for the Church today. The Bible gives many examples of prophecies that were spoken to give direction to the people of God. Prophets are first mentioned in the New Testament in Acts 11:

During this time some prophets traveled from Jerusalem to Antioch. One of them named Agabus stood up in one of the meetings and predicted by the Spirit that a great famine was coming upon the entire Roman world… (Acts 11:27-28).

Acts 13:1 mentions that the church in Antioch had "certain prophets and teachers" (KJV). Philip the evangelist "had four unmarried daughters who had the gift of prophecy" (Acts 21:9).

We again hear from Agabus when he warns Paul of persecution if he continues his journey to Jerusalem. He took Paul's belt and physically bound the apostle's hands and feet, and predicted, "The Holy Spirit declares, 'So shall the owner of this belt be bound by the Jewish leaders in Jerusalem and turned over to the Gentiles'" (Acts 21:11).

Although both of these messages had a foretelling element, many references to the New Testament prophets do not have a futuristic message. Rather, many inspired prophetic messages in the early church seemed to have the purpose of edifying the church:

Then Judas and Silas, both being prophets, spoke at length to the believers, encouraging and strengthening their faith (Acts 15:32)

But one who prophesies strengthens others, encourages them, and comforts them (1 Corinthians 14:3).

Timothy received a spiritual gift through a prophetic message when the elders laid their hands on him and prayed for him. Paul told Timothy to wage warfare with prophetic words given to him. "Timothy, my son, I give you this instruction in keeping with the prophecies once made about you, so that by following them you may fight the good fight" (1 Tim. 1:18 NIV).

Many times prophecies are confirmations of those things the Lord has already spoken to us in our hearts. At other times the Lord may use prophecy to give us clear direction for our lives. Either way, the prophecy must be in line with the Word of God and our spirit must affirm it.

When God says something prophetically about you, He is speaking out and releasing your potential.

When God says something prophetically about you, He is speaking out and releasing your potential. God is supernatural, and as Christians, we are supernatural as well because He lives within us. People today are hungry for the supernatural; you only have to look at the popular books and movies of our day to see this theme of supernatural events or people using supernatural powers. We believe God places this desire for the supernatural in us, yet the enemy is quick to take advantage and produces a counterfeit that draws people away from God, rather than closer to Him.

Prophetic Words Will Always Bring Us Closer to God

True prophetic words come from God and draw us closer to Him. They are edifying words that God speaks so we can hear Him not only for ourselves but also through others. Sometimes God will use a prophetic word to strengthen and refresh us in our walk with Him. Sometimes we can receive prophetic visions. Whatever way God chooses, His desire is to communicate with us. Our God is a master communicator.

"Inspired Preaching" Prophecy

Some call prophecy "inspired preaching." Indeed it is, but it is not limited to this arena. Most preachers know when they are preaching under a greater inspiration rather than just giving the information they have in their notes. The Holy Spirit can open our hearts to see deeper into the Scriptures. Like the facets on a diamond, the Word of God has many sides and beauties that only show up when they are in the light. The Holy Spirit can shine His light upon the Word of God and reveal some things we have never considered before.

As speakers, we have both experienced this many times over the years. There have been times when the Holy Spirit redirects us when we are teaching. We have our notes in hand, but just before the time comes for us to deliver the message, the Holy Spirit causes our mind to go in a different direction. Sometimes the Holy

Spirit directs us to turn to a particular passage. As we obey and open the Bible, there is a brand new message revealed to us. We did not get it by study, laboring over different translations or praying for revelation. It was a prophetic message that just fell into our spirit. It was not just a thought, but a whole message. These sometimes become life messages that have been preached over and over again. They are rich in revealing the heart of God and are timeless in their scope.

Gift of Prophecy in Operation

"Inspired preaching," however, is only one side of prophetic utterances. When the Holy Spirit gives us some spontaneous thoughts to express, the gift of prophecy is in operation. Like the other gifts of the Spirit, it is made possible by the supernatural operation of the Holy Spirit. My (Dennis') first encounter with the gift of prophecy is clear in my mind. I was attending a meeting of believers in a house, standing in a circle, praying with some of the people. I had my mind in the receptive mode because I wanted to hear from the Lord. As I stood with the others, just being in His presence, I had a thought. It was so unusual that I decided to speak it out. The word was simple—"Jesus said, 'Behold, I am standing in your midst.'"

A few moments later, the phone rang. The person on the other end said he had been in prayer for the meeting and had a vision. He was so excited; he just wanted to share it. He saw us standing in a circle praying, and standing in our midst was Jesus! You can imagine how my faith soared that night! I was learning to be sensitive to the Lord.

My first experience in receiving and giving a prophecy was with two Christian brothers in a small prayer meeting. My heart began to beat rapidly, and I (Larry) became aware that God was with us in a special way. I sensed God was going to give me a prophecy, so I asked the two brothers in Christ to pray for me. They prayed and a few moments later the Lord began to speak through me a prophetic message for us. This was new territory for me. Later on, as I grew in giving prophetic messages, I generally received a deep peace from the Lord and I opened my mouth and gave expression to the impressions I was receiving from the Lord.

Prophecy Edifies, Exhorts, and Comforts

The Bible tells us that when we prophesy, we are building up the Church (see 1 Cor. 14:5). We previously mentioned that "one who prophesies strengthens others, encourages them, and comforts them." We have often had people come to us after a meeting and confess that the prophetic word we had given particularly blessed them. They seemed to feel that it was personal, just for them. They were encouraged. Sometimes several would come and say the same thing. It is wonderful how the Lord can personalize His word to our hearts. When this happens to us, it makes us realize just how much the Lord cares for us. It is as though He takes the time out of running the universe to come down and speak a word to us. That is amazing grace!

Several years ago I (Dennis) was going through a rough patch. I was not sure just what the Lord was doing, but I thought that maybe He was through with me. In truth, I felt like quitting. I think we all face those seasons of discouragement. I have often felt like quitting on Monday mornings, but this was different. I was seriously thinking about it for the first time; I was even thinking of what I could do for a living. I was in a meeting with a prophet, and during the course of the week he had given me a very encouraging word about the will of God for my life. He had spoken in the future tense and that had blessed me because I was having trouble seeing a future for myself. A few days later I was in a different church, meeting with the local elders. During that meeting an elder spoke a simple word to me. It went something like this: "Dennis, I know you get discouraged sometimes, but the Lord is telling you not to quit. Do not give up; He is not finished with you." I went home more determined than ever to keep on going. I realized that God was not finished with me. I was just going through a time that would eventually pass.

When God speaks to us prophetically in this fashion, it has the power to release new faith and expectation in our hearts. Sometimes a single word can change the atmosphere. We move from fear to overcoming faith. What seemed so helpless and hopeless suddenly becomes a dim memory, if we remember it at all. God may not tell you your whole life's plan, but He will give you the courage and faith to take the next step.

Prophecy Should Be Tested

All prophecy needs to be tested, according to the Scriptures. "Do not stifle the Holy Spirit. Do not scoff at prophecies, but test everything that is said. Hold on to what is good" (1 Thess. 5:19-21). Testing a prophecy may mean we go to our pastor or other trusted Christian leader to present it to them and ask for their input.

Additionally, all prophecy must be tested by the Scriptures. If it does not line up with the Bible, do not receive it. Bible teacher Derek Prince says that not testing a prophecy is:

"...like turning a young person loose in a very fast sports car without checking the steering and the brakes. He may end up in a wreck. Over the years, I have seen scores and scores of wrecks through the misuse of prophecy. I have seen homes broken up, churches divided, and people ruined financially and in other ways through the wrong use of prophecy. Prophecy is an extremely powerful instrument, and if it is misused, it can be misused to the destruction of people."[1]

Prophetic Words Must Have God's Meaning and God's Timing

We must especially test a prophetic word for its meaning and timing. It may be for today or it may be for ten years in the future. We must be careful not to assume we know how and when to act upon a personal prophecy. I (Larry) learned this the hard way. Several years ago I had two prophetic messages spoken over me about being called to minister to young people just as I did over two decades ago. One prophetic message came from a pastor in Oregon and the other came from a Presbyterian pastor in New Zealand. I assumed from receiving these two nearly identical prophecies that I was to start a youth ministry, so I did. I began meeting with about 35 youth every week in my hometown.

Shortly thereafter, the Lord brought me into a relationship with some young leaders who had started a Bible study every Tuesday called "Tuesday Bible Study" (TBS). As our friendship grew, these leaders started to look to me as one of their spiritual advisors for their fledgling group. While the youth ministry I had started was declining (because it really wasn't in God's timing and I missed God's meaning) the TBS youth ministry was growing to over 1,000 young people!

I finally realized that I had missed the timing of God and He never wanted me immediately to start a new youth ministry. He called me to be a mentor to these young leaders. If I had waited to see what God was going to do with TBS, I wouldn't have started the other youth ministry. Timing is always a critical part of seeing a prophetic word come to pass. Getting the wrong timing for prophetic words is the most common error people make in processing prophecy.

Prophetic Words Must Be Confirmed in Our Hearts

Often we are tempted to add to the prophetic word. This usually brings confusion. A friend told me (Larry) of a prophetic word spoken to his wife and him that said, "I see children." Afterwards, people quickly speculated that they would soon be pregnant since they already had two children. The word never said "pregnancy," and later they saw this played out in how they had mentored a teenage mother in their home, like a "daughter."

If somebody tells you through a prophecy to go to the mission field, please don't quit your job unless you know that God has also spoken this same word to you and it is confirmed by the other ways the Lord speaks, such as through His peace, circumstances, and His still, small voice, for example. I've seen people get into horrible problems by trying to run their lives based on what other people told them was a "prophetic message from God."

If the prophecy you receive doesn't bear agreement in your heart, you often will know it by a lack of peace in your spirit. Something tells you things just are not quite right.

There are a lot of well-meaning people who think they are hearing from God for others, but the truth is they are not. If someone prophesies something to you that is not already in your heart, then I suggest you write down the words that are spoken over you and wait for the Lord to reveal to you whether or not the words are from Him. If it is from God, He will clearly show you.

Allow God to Speak to You Prophetically

Operating in any spiritual gift takes practice. Not many people will begin by prophesying perfectly. Paul said those with the gift of prophecy should, "prophesy in proportion to their faith" (see Romans 12:6). As we begin to prophesy, we will grow and mature in it.

Sometimes we may feel that we are only capable of receiving a little bit from the Lord. Our thoughts may start with "this is what the Lord is saying," or, "I had a thought that I think might be a blessing to someone." Prophecy, by its very nature, is usually very uplifting. The words will often be encouragement to the people. The Holy Spirit will remind us of a truth that we need to hear. When the Holy Spirit speaks in this way, there is a witness that occurs deep in our hearts. Something unique is released into our spirits by the Holy Spirit. It becomes a personal word to us. It is no longer some abstract, theoretical truth, but means something personal to our lives and circumstances.

When I feel an impression to give a prophetic message, I (Larry) ask myself these three questions: "Lord, is this from you?" "Lord, is this something you have given to me to share with others, or is it just for me to pray more effectively?" "Lord, is this for now or for later?"

There have been times when I have felt the Lord give me a prophetic message in a meeting, and I felt I should wait. Later, someone else gives the same message either through a prophecy and testimony or through a message from Scripture. This was affirming to me that I had heard from God.

We believe the Lord greatly desires to place His words in our mouths and speak through us prophetically to others. Jesus promises to "...give you the right words and such wisdom that none of your opponents will be able to reply or refute you" (Luke 21:15). If the Lord speaks a message in your spirit that you believe is a true prophecy for someone else, be careful not to be presumptuous when giving it to the individual. As much as is possible, try to have the individual's spiritual leaders involved in this process so they can help the person discern the meaning of the prophecy.

After I (Larry) give an individual a prophetic message, I usually say something like: "I sense the Lord may be saying…" rather than "thus says the Lord." We often turn people off by our super-spiritual mannerisms, our traditions, or by our personalities. I sometimes encounter older ministers who prophesy in King James English. It is unclear to me why someone getting a word from God would choose to speak like they did during the King James era; however, perhaps it is best to look beyond the language used and the vessel God has chosen in order to concentrate on the word of the Lord.

You could say that a prophecy is like a clear, clean refreshing stream of water from the Lord; however, the channel or person who gives the prophetic message is like a hose. So we should not be surprised when we encounter a problem: the prophecy may taste a bit like the hose! We must discern between the message from the Lord and the hose—the person giving the message.

God wants us to be encouraged with prophecies that help us to know Him better. We can trust that, as His sheep, we will learn to recognize His voice, all the while remembering that prophecy is just one of the ways God speaks to us; it should not be used exclusively to hear from God. Nevertheless, let's continue to seek Him and keep our hearts open as He speaks prophetic words that help refresh our walk with Him. God wants us to be full of the Holy Spirit's anointing and to operate in spiritual gifts. He wants to bless people through us. He wants to reach out through our lives to encourage and exhort others.

Endnote

[1] Derek Prince, *The Gifts of the Spirit* (Kensington, PA: Whitaker House, 2007), 205.

Chapter 10

Distinguishing Between Spirits

*...to another **distinguishing between spirits***
(1 Corinthians 12:10 NIV).

Since we both travel frequently, we often need to use hotel rooms. Many times when we enter the room we can discern if there is a demonic spirit in the room due to the last guests who used the room. How do we know? Through the supernatural gift of distinguishing between, or the discerning of, spirits. It only takes a short time to cleanse the room by the blood of Jesus and the name of Jesus. The Bible tells us, "They overcame him (the enemy) by the blood of the Lamb and by the word of their testimony" (Rev. 12:11).

This gift does not refer only to discerning of evil spirits. It could also refer to discerning when the Holy Spirit is present. Or it could refer to discerning the faith that is in the human spirit. For example, in Acts 14, we have an example of Paul discerning faith in a man who was crippled (see Acts 14:8-10). Paul was in the middle of speaking when he looked at the one man in the group and saw faith in him. He stopped in the middle of his message and said, "Stand up straight on your feet!" The man responded in faith and began to walk. This was not an instance of Paul discerning the

Holy Spirit or the working of evil spirits, but rather the spirit of faith that was in this man.

Another example of the use of the gift of discerning of spirits was when Jesus met a woman who was bent over because she was plagued by a spirit of infirmity for eighteen years. Jesus said to her, "Woman, you are loosed from your infirmity" (Luke 13:12 NKJV). Jesus discerned that this infirmity was caused by a demonic spirit. He laid His hands on her, and immediately she straightened up and glorified God, set free from this spirit of infirmity.

Other Biblical Examples

Peter received God's gift of discernment, which enabled him to see through the deception of Ananias and Sapphira, who had sold some property and brought only part of the money to the apostles, claiming it was the full amount.

> *Then Peter said, "Ananias, why have you let satan fill your heart? You lied to the Holy Spirit, and you kept some of the money for yourself. The property was yours to sell or not sell, as you wished. And after selling it, the money was also yours to give away. How could you do a thing like this? You weren't lying to us but to God!"* (Acts 5:3-4).

In Philippi, a girl followed Paul around shouting, "These men are servants of the Most High God, and they have come to tell you how to be saved." Paul discerned that she had a demon in her and immediately cast it out (see Acts 16:17).

Something Doesn't Smell Right

One time, at a gathering of young people in the home of a Christian single mom and her teenage daughters, I (Dennis) had an unusual experience. As I stood in the dining room, two unfamiliar young men walked by me, and as they did I had a peculiar sensation arise within my spirit. I felt decidedly uncomfortable. I did not know what this meant, but it set me praying as I watched them and listened to what they were saying.

I know that this is a very subjective kind of experience. Just a feeling alone is not enough. It is too easy to be wrong, but when we watch and pray, when we listen to what is really being said, the Holy Spirit can warn us of unseen entrapments. After all, the Bible says that satan often appears as an angel of light. We must have more than feelings, good or bad. We need more than the appearance of spirituality; we need to know the operating principles by which a person is living. In short, we need to hear their theology and their testimony to know for sure.

Some might confuse this with being critical of another, but that is not the case. It is not suspecting a person to be a certain way when he is not. I could not criticize these young men in any way, since I did not know them or know anything about them. I simply felt an uncomfortable sensation when they passed nearby. As I waited and prayed I overheard them speaking about their background and their belief. They were a part of a cult group that went about looking for weak sheep they could draw away. I will not name them, but suffice it to say they drew a number of my friends away. The end was not good for those who left and followed these false believers. In fact, they all returned and told the sad tale of what had transpired.

Have you heard the old saying "something doesn't smell right around here"? That is what I felt like. I couldn't put my finger on what was wrong, but I knew something was not right. As I pressed into the Holy Spirit in prayer, He showed me the problem. How many times does the Holy Spirit try to warn of dangers in the road ahead and we just ignore it? We may even feel guilty for having such negative feelings toward someone. If we will just pray in the

Spirit and ask the Holy Spirit to reveal the reason for the uneasiness, He will most certainly show us. It is for our sake that this is happening. He is fulfilling His mission and is leading us into truth. He is protecting us from error. It follows that we need to be biblical scholars. We need to store the word in our hearts. The Bible is the standard of belief and life. If someone is advocating something that violates the principles found in the Word of God, we must not listen to them; we may even need to confront them in love.

The Power to Speak the Supernatural Mind of God

Distinguishing between spirits is one of the discerning gifts giving us the "power to know." It also gives us the power to say or speak the supernatural mind of God so that others will look to Him. With the gift of discerning of spirits, we can see or understand even that which is hidden or obscure.

I recall ministering in a home one night that was packed with people. As I was ministering, I came under an attack from satan. Unbelief was a tangible force in the room that night. The Holy Spirit spoke to me that there was someone present who was under the power of a demon of unbelief. I shared this with the people. The Holy Spirit offered deliverance. No one responded. I was in faith and made a bold declaration. I bound that spirit in the name of Jesus and commanded it to release the person. Then I went on speaking.

Distinguishing between spirits is one of the discerning gifts giving us the "power to know." It also gives us the power to say or speak the supernatural mind of God so that others will look to Him.

Later, the pastor's wife told me what she saw happen. There was a visitor present who had come to visit the family in whose home the meetings were being held. Not feeling friendly toward these "charismatic crazies," she felt stuck in a meeting she did not want to attend. When I bound the spirit of unbelief, the pastor's wife happened to glance at the visitor and saw her begin to cry when she was set free. The demon of unbelief within her was trying to stop the power of God, but the Lord turned the tables on it!

There have been other occasions when the Holy Spirit within me warned me about ministries and ministers. I was invited to be a part of a ministry team one time, but soon after arriving there, I began to sense that something was wrong. Everything sounded and looked right, but my spirit was waving a flag.

If you have watched any American football then you know what a flagged play is. When the referee sees a problem, he throws a flag onto the field. The whole game stops until things are sorted out. The Holy Spirit can flag the play, too. When we sense the Holy Spirit urging caution, we should begin immediately to pray for insight.

As I prayed, the Holy Spirit told me to leave that ministry. It was not until much later that I discovered the reason for my lack of peace. We should not just act on a whim or a feeling, but when we lose our peace, we had better find out why.

Reading Between the Lines to Distinguish Truth

Scripture contains many exhortations for Christians to test all teaching. John writes, "Dear friends, do not believe everyone who claims to speak by the Spirit. You must test them to see if the spirit they have comes from God. For there are many false prophets in the world" (1 John 4:1). This gift is not a gift of suspicion where you suspect a person of being a certain way when he is not that way at all. With the gift of discerning of spirits you have the ability to read between the lines and distinguish between truth and error. Through this supernatural gift God enables you to perceive genuine motives from false ones and recognize inconsistencies between words and deeds. Obviously, we always need to pray and ask our heavenly Father for wisdom before we speak out to identify any deception.

 With the gift of discerning of spirits you have the ability to read between the lines and distinguish between truth and error.

In the next two chapters we will discuss two precious gifts of the Holy Spirit that are often misunderstood; the gift of speaking in tongues and the gift of interpretation of tongues.

Chapter 11

Different Kinds of Tongues

*...to another speaking in **different kinds of tongues*** (1 Corinthians 12:10 NIV).

Since the gift of tongues in this chapter and the gift of interpretation of tongues in the next chapter work together, let's begin with some basic definitions. These definitions are not intended to be all-encompassing, but rather practical introductions. Note that the words "to speak" are central to each one. Speaking in different kinds of tongues is the ability given by the Holy Spirit to speak in a language not understood by the speaker. Interpretation of tongues is the ability given by the Holy Spirit to speak in a language understood by the speaker, the meaning of words previously spoken in an unknown language. There are many kinds of tongues. For example, the Bible speaks of tongues that are a personal prayer language from us to the Lord, a tongue that is a foreign language not known to the one who is speaking, or the tongues of angels (see 1 Cor. 13). Sometimes speaking in "tongues" is called speaking in "spiritual languages."

In Ephesus, some of the believers had never even heard of the Holy Spirit. So Paul instructed them, telling how they could receive the Holy Spirit. When he prayed for them, the Holy Spirit came upon them and they spoke in spiritual languages. "...when

Paul laid his hands on them, the Holy Spirit came on them, and they spoke in other tongues..." (Acts 19:6).

 Speaking in a spiritual language is a direct line of communication between your spirit and God.

Often, when believers are filled with the Holy Spirit, they begin to speak in *tongues* or a new heavenly language. The Bible says they magnify God (see Acts 10:46). This personal prayer language is understood by God because it is your spirit speaking to God. Speaking in a spiritual language is a direct line of communication between your spirit and God. In the Book of Acts, speaking in tongues was often the initial outward sign accompanying the infilling of the Holy Spirit.

Charging Your Spiritual Battery

God wants us to build ourselves up in faith so we may be His witnesses. In Acts 1:8 we read that when the Holy Spirit comes upon us, we will receive power to be His witnesses. Praying in tongues builds us up spiritually. It's like charging your spiritual battery. You can, with power, pray for the sick, and minister to people and help them as you continue to build up yourself spiritually by praying in a spiritual language.

Speaking in tongues has been controversial in some parts of the church of Jesus Christ. One of the first times that I (Larry) went to a public meeting where I was told that some of the people spoke in tongues, I sat near the back of the building. I wanted to make a quick exit if I became too uncomfortable! Although some believers hesitate because they have heard or seen misuses of the gift of tongues or other gifts of the Spirit, we have no need to be afraid.

It seems funny to recall now, but one of the fears that I had when I was considering being filled with the Holy Spirit was that I would be in a place like a department store and the Spirit of God would come on me. I was afraid I'd begin to speak in a spiritual language uncontrollably. Then one day I read this Scripture, "Remember that people who prophesy are in control of their spirit..." (1 Cor. 14:32). Your spirit is subject to you. It's like a water spigot. You turn it off and on. The water is always there, but it's under your control. You choose to pray or not to pray in tongues at any given time, but it's God who gives you the gift and the power to speak.

Bypassing the Devil

We pray two ways—with our mind and with our spirit. Both are needed, and both are under the influence of the Holy Spirit, according to First Corinthians 14:14-15:

For if I pray in tongues, my spirit is praying, but I don't understand what I am saying. Well then, what shall I do? I will pray in the spirit, and I will also pray in words I understand. I will sing in the spirit, and I will also sing in words I understand (1 Corinthians 14:14-15).

The first way we pray is with our mind. When we pray, "Our Father in Heaven...," it's coming from our mind. We understand it. We are using our intellect to pray in a learned language. The second way we pray is with our spirit. When we pray with our spirit (in tongues), it's unfruitful to our mind. Our spirit is praying directly to the Father without having to accept the limitations of our human intellect.

In other words, when you and I pray with our spirit, we have no idea what we are saying, but our heavenly Father knows what we're saying. We come in simple faith and trust God to provide the form of the words and their meaning to Him. Using our new language, we edify ourselves or "build ourselves up" spiritually (see 1 Cor. 14:4). It is like a direct phone line to God. We both pray in tongues daily, because when we pray in our spiritual languages, we bypass the devil. He has no idea what we are saying. We are speaking the "language of angels" and "mysteries" according to the Bible (see 1 Cor. 13:1;14:2).

How important is it for us as Christians to speak in spiritual languages? Paul the apostle wished that every person spoke in tongues and stressed that the gift of tongues was an important part of his spiritual life. "I wish you could all speak in tongues…I thank God that I speak in tongues more than any of you" (1 Cor. 14:5; 14:18).

Is someone a second-rate Christian if they don't speak in a spiritual language? No, of course not! But God wants us to be blessed and use these blessings so we can fulfill His call on our lives. Some say they believe it is selfish to pray in tongues. Is it selfish to pray? Is it selfish to read the Bible? Why do we pray and read the Scriptures and speak in spiritual languages? We do it to communicate with God and in order to be built up spiritually so we can be effective in helping other people.

My (Dennis') first experience with tongues and interpretation was in a church service. I distinctly remember standing in the congregation during the Sunday evening service, and there was a quiet pause in the worship. While standing there, worshiping God, I felt an overwhelming sense of His presence. Inside, I felt *full*. I needed to do something to express this *fullness*.

I did not know what to do to relieve this great inner pressure, so I spoke out in tongues. After a few moments, the pastor gave the interpretation. It then occurred to me that I had just given a "message in tongues."

You must understand that I had first spoken in tongues just the night before. I was not a seasoned veteran, I was just a beginner. It did not matter; the Holy Spirit was willing to use me to speak! It was all very exciting. I was actually experiencing God in modern day life! There were many subsequent times when I experienced that same feeling of fullness and that same awesome presence. In fact, I began to look for that presence and to prepare myself for it. As I learned to yield, it became easier to do so.

Tongues for Our Personal Devotional Life

Tongues are an underrated gift. It is easy to make light of something we may not understand. There are different uses for this powerful gift. The most important aspect of tongues is for our own personal devotional life. We can speak in tongues in our prayer language with which we edify ourselves (see 1 Cor. 14:4). Paul did not diminish this important gift, saying, "I thank God that I speak in tongues more than any of you" (1 Cor. 14:18). He expressed how tongues were extremely useful in his prayer life. Jude tells us that when we pray in the Spirit, or in tongues, that we are actually building ourselves up in the holy faith (see Jude 1:20). We both pray in tongues a lot, especially when preparing for ministry and preparing a message to preach.

 The most important aspect of tongues is for our own personal devotional life.

I (Dennis) have a friend in the ministry who was vacationing in the mountains. On his way back to South Florida, while driving at night, he felt the need to pray. He did not know what the need was so he just prayed in tongues. As he drove down the Florida Turnpike late that night, a car approached from the rear. As it passed he heard a loud noise and something hit his car. He stopped at the next service plaza to look at his car. He didn't see anything until the next day. Someone had shot at his car and the bullet had hit the little strip of metal that held the windshield in place. It saved his life. At that time several had been killed in this fashion on the turnpike. God had protected him. His time of praying in tongues had prevailed for him and his wife.

Tongues That Minister to Others in Their Own Language

The Scriptures talk of different kinds of tongues. There are different uses for tongues. I have experienced this in my own life. I remember several times in which the Holy Spirit opened my mouth to talk to people of other languages. One in particular stands out. A Hispanic brother in a church in North Florida spoke English with no problem, but as I began to prophesy over him I heard myself speaking in tongues. Spanish began to pour out of my mouth. He was very excited about the word and said, "If that comes to pass I will be a wealthy man." I inquired what the word was about and he told me it was about cattle. He was a cowboy, which I did not know. Several years later I saw him again. He affirmed that the word had indeed come to pass.

I have had a number of occasions when the Holy Spirit would allow me to speak to someone in their native tongue. This is not something I can turn on or off. It is in the hands of the Holy Spirit. It has happened as I speak to an individual and it has happened in a congregational setting. One time I gave a message in tongues under the inspiration of the Holy Spirit. There was a brother there who spoke perfect Spanish. He translated the word for the congregation.

That is not how the gift of interpretation of tongues usually works, but it was amazing to witness.

A message in tongues often sounds like prophecy, and they are frequently words of encouragement and faith. Sometimes they sound like one of the Psalms—beautiful words of love and devotion that might have been penned by David himself. It is a beautiful thing to hear the human spirit expressing its devotion to the Lord our God in a language that could be described as poetic.

These declaration gifts are extremely useful and powerful in communicating the heart of God to a congregation, or an individual. I remember one time I was in Guadalajara, Mexico. I was part of a team that was having an outdoors meeting with an evangelist. Many miracles and healings were happening. People were being healed of cancerous tumors, blind eyes were being opened, and the deaf were hearing. Lame people were throwing away their crutches and canes. It was a wonderful time with Jesus.

I had been praying that I might be released to speak to some Mexican people in their own language, but nothing had happened. It wasn't until the crusade was over and we were packing up, that the Holy Spirit released me in this fashion. There were two small children standing around and watching us break down the platform. I approached them and began to speak in Spanish to them. Their little faces lit up with joy and they began to shake their heads in agreement. They left with great joy upon their countenances. I do not know what I said, but that is unimportant. It was not for me, it was for them, and it was wonderful.

We have learned that if we will just listen and be open to the Holy Spirit, He will speak something to us for the people. It may be a prophecy; it may be a tongue or an interpretation of a tongue. The key is learning to listen, or to pay attention to the thoughts that come into our mind and our spirit. That is where we hear, in our mind and our spirit. The words come into our mind and we can process them with the Holy Spirit's help. We can decide whether or not we will articulate them. We filter them through the Word of God. If they fail the Scripture test, then we will not say them. God may be old, but He is not confused! He will not say something that is contrary to Scripture.

As we maintained earlier, some may argue that these gifts passed away with the apostle John, but that stance is completely unbiblical. The Bible says that tongues will cease when "perfection comes" (1 Cor. 13:10 NIV). Some people believe that this means tongues are no longer needed today. They believe that "perfection" refers to the Bible. They fail to realize that the same passage says we shall see "face to face." We will not see the *Bible* face to face. We will see *Jesus* face to face. At that time, at the end of the age, there will be no need for the gift of tongues. But until we see Jesus face to face, the Lord has given us the gifts of tongues, prophecy, and other supernatural gifts of the Holy Spirit to use for His glory here on earth.

Do not try to interpret the Bible through your experiences, the opinions of others, or through what makes sense to you. Let the Bible speak for itself and believe what it says. It is simple, direct, and written so that the common man can understand it. The Holy Spirit will make these truths evident to you as you ask Him and trust Him. We have found it useful to pray like this: "Holy Spirit, if these things are true we want to know. Please reveal the truth to us in a way that we can understand. Amen."

Chapter 12

Interpretation of Tongues

*...and to still another the **interpretation of tongues*** (1 Corinthians 12:10 NIV).

As we mentioned in the last chapter, different kinds of tongues and interpretation of tongues are two supernatural gifts of the Spirit that function together. Again, the interpretation of tongues is the ability given by the Holy Spirit to speak, in a language understood by the speaker, the meaning of words previously spoken in an unknown language. Indeed, the gift of interpretation of tongues is dependent upon the gift of tongues in order to operate. During such times, the outcome of the dual manifestation is similar to the gift of prophecy. The interpreted message edifies and exhorts the Church, while it also gives glory to God. The word "interpret" means *to expound and lay open what is concealed from the understanding.*[1] We both have been used by God with the gift of the interpretation of the gift of tongues on various occasions. I (Dennis) usually hear the words in English in my mind. As I hear them, or see them, I just speak them out in English.

Interpretation is usually not an exact translation of the message in tongues but rather a general meaning of the words spoken. It is passing on the meaning in a way that can be understood. Sometimes the interpretation of tongues seems longer or shorter than the actual message in tongues. It often depends on the person conveying the message. Some people are wordier than others and will use more words to convey the same meaning. It is possible, however, for an interpretation to be a literal translation. For example, a person gives an interpretation in a language he doesn't know which is verified by someone who knows the language and hears an accurate word-for-word translation.

 Interpretation is usually not an exact translation of the message in tongues but rather a general meaning of the words spoken.

The Bible says we should be eager to have the special abilities the Spirit gives. We should seek those abilities that will strengthen the whole Church. The gift of interpretation helps to strengthen the Church because more people can understand. "So anyone who speaks in tongues should pray also for the ability to interpret what has been said" (1 Cor. 14:13).

Sometimes we can be fearful when beginning to move in these gifts. There is no need to fear. Remember what Jesus told His disciples:

You fathers—if your children ask for a fish, do you give them a snake instead? Or if they ask for an egg, do you give them a scorpion? Of course not! So if you sinful people know how to give good gifts to your children, how much more will your heavenly Father give the Holy Spirit to those who ask Him (Luke 11:11-13).

If you are a child of God, and you are prompted or stirred to ask for a certain gift of the Holy Spirit, you are to ask for it, and you will receive what you ask for.

Lester Sumrall tells the story of a time he preached in Washington, DC. After his sermon, one brother in Christ gave a message in tongues and another interpreted. When they had finished, a young man walked to the front and spoke in a foreign language to the one who had given the message. The brother answered, "I'm sorry, sir, but I don't understand any other language."

The man replied, "But you spoke my language beautifully. I am Persian. You spoke my language and told me that I must get right with God, and that I must find God right now."

The brother answered, "No, it was the Spirit who spoke to you. It was God talking to you, not me." Much to that young man's surprise, neither of the two men—the one who gave the message in tongues nor the one who interpreted it—could speak or understand his language. He stood there, trembling, then knelt down and gave his heart to the Lord Jesus Christ. That night the gifts of tongues and interpretation were magnificently fulfilled. Just as the Bible says, it was a sign to the unbeliever. God spoke to that man in the Persian language through two men when neither of them understood a foreign tongue.[2]

Tongues to Build Up the Church

In First Corinthians 12:28-30, God mentions that He has appointed some in the Church for various tasks and responsibilities.

Here are some of the parts God has appointed for the church: first are apostles, second are prophets, third are teachers, then those who do miracles, those who have the gift of healing, those who can help others, those who have the gift of leadership, those who speak in unknown languages. Are we all apostles? Are we all prophets? Are we all teachers? Do we all have the power to do miracles? Do we all have the gift of healing? Do we all have the ability to speak in unknown languages?

Do we all have the ability to interpret unknown languages? Of course not! (1 Corinthians 12:28-30)

Because this Scripture states, "Do we all have the ability to speak in unknown languages?" many think this means that not all can speak in tongues as a personal prayer language. However, this Scripture is really asking, "Are all appointed to speak with the gift of tongues *to the Church?*"

You see, there is a gift to be used *in the Church* which is a type of speaking in tongues. It is different from the type of speaking in tongues that we experience when we pray in our prayer language. When this gift of tongues is used in the Church, someone who has the gift gives a message in tongues, and someone with the *gift of interpretation* gives the meaning, thus building up the Body of Christ.

So, although you may speak in tongues so you can be built up spiritually to serve God better, you may also sometimes receive a special gift of tongues and/or interpretation of tongues to be used to build up His Church.

To Be Used in Love

After Paul lists the ministry gifts of the Holy Spirit to the Church in First Corinthians 12:28-30, he says in verse 31, "...eagerly desire the greater gifts. And now I will show you the most excellent way (NIV)."

What is the greater gift? The greater gift depends on the situation you're in. If you need healing, you believe God for the "greater" gift of healing because that is what you need. What is the "most excellent way"? It is love. Chapter 13 of First Corinthians tells us all about it! Some say they don't need all these gifts; they just need love. That's not what Paul was trying to communicate.

He is emphasizing that to possess spiritual gifts without love amounts to nothing. We need to use these gifts in love.

Use Your Tools!

The Holy Spirit will reveal many things to us if we are willing to allow Him to place us in a position where the needs of the people cause us to draw upon His grace and power. If we are content just to occupy space we will probably not see much of this in our lives. These gifts are not for showing off or for bragging about, they are for ministering to people.

If you were a carpenter, you would undoubtedly have a toolbox full of useful tools with which to engage in your trade. You would know which tool was best for the job and would do your best to have anything you might need on hand to complete your project. These gifts of the Holy Spirit are tools for ministry. The Holy Spirit is the one who will reach into the toolbox and pull out the tool that you need. We have found ourselves moving in and out of different gifts as the needs of the people changed. You can move from prophecy, to word of knowledge, to gifs of healing, to the gift of miracles all in the space of few minutes time.

Do not put yourself in a box. Determine that you are going to experience the move of the Holy Spirit in your own life and ministry. These gifts are not just for a chosen few, but are there for any who desire them. The more you are willing to be a front-line person, the more you will see happen. If you wanted to be a lifeguard, you would be close to the water, not back in the parking lot somewhere. If you wanted to become a tennis pro, you would buy the gear and practice hard on the courts. You would probably take some lessons and you would play a lot. Just watching the game and reading the magazines would not be enough. It takes action to accomplish these things. It takes a willingness to be useful to the

Lord. The Holy Spirit will teach you and will bring others into your life to teach you. He will show you those who are ahead of you in the faith. They will be living examples of what you can accomplish. It all starts with you and your desires to be used by the Holy Spirit.

 These gifts are not just for a chosen few, but are there for any who desire them.

Now let's get really practical. How do we live, day-by-day, supernaturally natural? Remember, these gifts are not just for a chosen few, but they are for all of us to use to bring glory to God. They are for housewives, and lawyers, and assembly line workers, and students, and for everyone from all walks of life. In the next chapters we will focus on how we can experience these supernatural spiritual gifts operating in our lives both in the church and in everyday life.

Endnotes

[1] Noah Webster, *American Dictionary of the English Language (1828)* (Chesapeake, VA: Foundation for American Christian Education, 1967).

[2] Lester Sumrall, *The Gifts and Ministries of the Holy Spirit* (New Kensington, PA: Whitaker House, 1982), 128-129.

Part III

Using Your Supernatural Gifts

Chapter 13

Actively Waiting for God

*I*t was a hot July day in central Maine. My friend Robin and I (Dennis) made our way into Bangor. Our plan was to go to the Maine State Employment office and get a job for the summer. We arrived to find a room filled with folding chairs on one side and desks occupied with various people on the other. We found a seat, which wasn't too hard since we were the only ones there besides the secretaries.

One lady observed our presence and asked if she could help us. My response was a classic, "We are just waiting for something to happen." I remember the look on her face. I am sure she noticed the hayseeds behind our ears. She just shook her head and with a sad smile said, "It doesn't work that way; you will have to fill out some forms." That day proved pretty unfruitful as far as getting a job was concerned, but I will always remember the event. It was a life lesson for me.

Expectantly Waiting

The Scriptures teach us to "wait on the Lord." But what does "waiting" mean? We believe that many are just sitting around, sitting on a chair or in a pew, waiting for God to do something! We hate to be the bearer of bad news, but it doesn't work that way; you have to do something. There may not be any forms to fill out, but there are some valid biblical principles that we must learn.

Waiting is not being in a state of suspended limbo of inactivity. "Waiting" means "confident expectation" and it involves doing the things we can without running ahead of God. For example, if we need a job, we first need to pray, but then we need to pursue a job by putting together a resume, submitting applications, and going to employment agencies. We don't expect an employer to come knocking at our door while we sit and do nothing.

 "Waiting" means "confident expectation" and it involves doing the things we can without running ahead of God.

As an itinerant minister, I eat a lot of meals at restaurants. When you eat out you appreciate a place with good food and good service. I have been in some places where I seemed to be invisible. No one came to my table. I actually had to ask, "Is anyone working in this section"? Of course, the other extreme is where the one serving you is some sort of frustrated stand-up comedian who insists on inserting himself into your day.

I appreciate someone who tends to my needs without being intrusive. I like it when I do not have to wait forever to be served. It is great when the coffee cup isn't empty while I eat. I do not like getting the catsup after the food is gone. I guess you are getting the picture. They that wait upon the preacher get a good tip! That means they are going to have to observe my needs. They are watchful of my water glass and my coffee cup. They can tell when I am ready for dessert or the bill. Waiters actively "wait" on you by actively doing something.

If we carry that analogy to our waiting upon the Lord we begin to see the picture a little more clearly.

Power to Live a Life Pleasing to the Father

In the fifth chapter of John, Jesus healed the man at the pool of Bethesda. It caused a monumental stirring of the religious spirits in attendance. After all, it was the Sabbath Day. Who would ever think that God would do anything on that day? When Jesus was confronted by the angry legal experts, he made some astounding statements. Let us read them as they come from the Bible.

So Jesus explained, "I tell you the truth, the Son can do nothing by Himself. He does only what He sees the Father doing. Whatever the Father does, the Son also does. For the Father loves the Son and shows Him everything He is doing. In fact, the Father will show Him how to do even greater works than healing this man. Then you will truly be astonished" (John 5:19-20).

These are amazing statements. What did Jesus mean? Did he really mean that he could not do anything without the Father? I believe that Jesus meant just that. Jesus was totally committed to the will of God. He was not on the earth to do His own thing. The Bible is clear; Jesus left His authority and power in Heaven when he came to earth. He was living as a normal man. He was reliant upon the leadership of the Holy Spirit for everything. Granted, Jesus did not sin and He was not hampered with the unregenerate flesh of the First Adam, but He relied upon the Father for everything.

If Jesus, who was God, depended upon the Father for everything, how much more must we? Other than the event at the Temple (Luke 2:41-51), we know of no other events that would show that Jesus was anything other than a normal person. It was not until after He was baptized by John and was filled with the Holy Spirit that Jesus began His supernatural ministry.

How did Jesus live the life He did? How was He able to perform miracles and healings and deal compassionately with those around Him? The answer reveals the secret that God intends for us to walk in as well: Jesus was the man that He was because the Holy Spirit came upon Him and gave Him power to live a life that was pleasing to the Father. Jesus was a man who spent a lot of time in the Father's presence. He often spent the whole night in prayer. He was able to be moved by the Spirit of God. He was at rest and comfortable in that arena. He was setting an example for us to follow in His footsteps. Jesus could have been born, gone to the Cross, and been resurrected. These ministry years did not add to our redemption. He did this to show us how to continue on in the work He started. God is still working, and He wants us to enter into that work as Jesus did.

Waiting and Listening to the Holy Spirit

It is imperative to wait and see and hear in the Spirit. God has created us with certain abilities. One of the greatest natural gifts we have is that of imagination. We enjoy many things in our lives because someone had an idea. They could visualize something and wouldn't rest until what they saw became reality. I (Dennis) remember moving into an apartment one time. It was rather in need of a makeover. My wife said, "We will never be able to do this," but I had a vision. I knew that with a little work that place would be transformed. We are often overwhelmed by the challenges of life, but someone with a vision is able to see beyond the problems. They roll up their sleeves and get to work. That can often make the difference.

It is imperative to wait and see and hear in the Spirit.

What can we do to roll up our spiritual sleeves and get to work? We will share a few things we have learned along the way. We do not claim to know it all or have all the revelation, but we have learned some things that have consistently worked over the years.

Learning to Listen, Look, and Obey

The first thing we learned is that God creates the "Hearing Ear" and the "Seeing Eye." That is in the Bible. Proverbs 20:12 (NASB) says, "The hearing ear and the seeing eye, the Lord has made both of them." The thought expressed is not just the normal function of seeing and hearing, as wonderful as that is, but understanding what we hear and discerning what we see. We must learn to look and to listen to the Holy Spirit. Many times, He has an agenda of His own. If we are willing to look and listen and then obey, we will be a part of something supernatural.

Many years ago I (Dennis) learned how to do this. I was a part of a group of young people, high school through college age, which met at a home in Palm Springs, Florida. We would have wonderful worship together and share testimonials and Scriptures. In that setting I found that if I would pray in tongues and press into the presence of the Lord (I call that the secret place), He would reveal something to me. I was always asking Him if there was anything that He wanted me to share or to do to bless anyone. Without fail I would receive something. It may have been a verse that had been opened to me, or perhaps a testimony to encourage the believers. The point is, I learned to listen and then to wait for the timing to release what the Spirit had deposited in my heart. I later discovered that God could tell me other things. I began to prophesy, give messages in tongues, interpretation of tongues, words of knowledge, experience the gift of faith, gifts of healing, discernment of spirits, and words of wisdom. In short, whatever the Holy Spirit wanted to do, I was willing to be an accomplice.

Stepping Out

We must learn to listen, but it isn't always easy to obey. When we move out of the safety of the flock we become visible to others. Many of us do not want to be visible. We like the safety of being a part of the crowd. God wants to lift us up and use us to bring glory to His Son. If we are truly interested in seeing Jesus glorified, we will have to give up our right to invisibility. We will have to be willing to stand up and testify. We will have to lift our voice and allow the Holy Spirit to speak a word through us. We will have to be willing to lay our hands upon someone and declare the word of the Lord. We will have to release the word of healing the Holy Spirit gives to us.

In the early days of my (Dennis) ministry, my wife, Jeannie, and I had been invited to tour with a group of young people. We went about ministering in worship choruses and sharing testimonials. One evening, in New Orleans, Louisiana, we were on the platform sharing some worship. I was playing the guitar, praying a lot in tongues and asking the Lord for something to share. All of a sudden I had a thought. I know that all thoughts in my head are not from God, but this one was. He was very clear: "There is someone here with a bad left knee. If that individual will stand, I will heal the individual." That was pretty simple, but scary too. There is nothing vague about a word like that. There was no hiding in obscurity with that word. It was either God or it was not! I remember how I paced back and forth. I was sort of like Gideon and his fleece. "Lord, make the fleece dry and the ground wet. Okay, now make the fleece wet and the ground dry! How about turning the fleece inside out?" I knew that I had to make a decision with this word.

I finally decided to take a risk, but was unable to bring myself to say "left knee." That was so specific, and my faith was not up to that, so I just said "knee." Everyone on the team just looked at me. I was on the spot for sure. Finally someone stood up, and I breathed a great sigh of relief only to find out her purpose for standing was unrelated to my word of knowledge. After that person had her say, another lady stood and confessed that she was the one. I then asked her if it was the "left knee." She affirmed that it was. Faith soared in my heart at that moment. I instructed her to do something she couldn't do before. She knelt down to the floor and was immediately healed by the power of God.

Looking back, that was such a small thing, but it was a monumental thing to me. The group looked at me differently from then on. God was establishing me and I did not even know it. There have been countless words of knowledge over the years. There have been wonderful times of seeing God release His blessings into needy people. Sometimes I see little pictures that play in my mind. I get flashes of inspiration from the Holy Spirit.

Demystifying the Supernatural
Becoming Supernaturally Natural

We believe that God has called us, not just to minister this way to others, but to be a role model for others. He has called us to demystify the supernatural. He has sent us to show people how simple it is to move in the Holy Spirit. It starts with a desire. It begins when we say, "Lord, use me; I am willing to take a risk if it will bring glory to Your Name."

We are to be eager to have these gifts functioning in our lives. First Corinthians 14:1 says, "Let love be your highest goal! But you should also desire the special abilities the Spirit gives—especially the ability to prophesy." The word "desire" can actually mean to covet. We are not to just sit and say, "I hope God does something today." We are to press into the presence of God and insist, "Lord, use me. I am willing for You to do whatever You desire through me today. I will speak; I will pray; I will prophesy." God is looking for people just like that.

When we use the phrase, "I heard the Lord speak to me," we mean that we had a thought. We must admit that we have noticed that when God speaks to us this way, He sounds an awful lot like us. When we say, "God showed me a vision," we mean we saw something in our mind. Have you ever had a thought and then said, "That is just me"? Later you discovered that it wasn't just you, but the Lord had actually put that thought in your mind. We have asked this question many times and have had most people raise their hands in confession to this fact. We would greatly benefit if we become skillful in the Word of God. That can help us sort out truth from fantasy. We need to be masters of the principles of life found in the Bible.

Holy Spirit-Inspired Ideas

God has created us for this purpose. He has designed you and me to know Him, to walk with Him, to hear His voice and to see Him in our lives. We just need to understand how He does it. If you have been born again and especially if you have received the baptism of the Holy Spirit, you will be able to do these things. Even the lost are able to hear from God; how else do we come to Christ for salvation? Jesus tells us, "My sheep listen to My voice..." (John 10:27). We are encouraging you to listen.

God Uses Imperfect People

You may feel unworthy of being used by God. Who hasn't? The Greek word for *gifts* in First Corinthians 12 is *charisma*. The word *charisma* is derived from the Greek noun *charis*. *Charis* is normally translated as *grace*. Grace is defined as "the unmerited favor of God toward the undeserving and the ill-deserving."[1] There is nothing in ourselves that causes us to deserve these gifts, but God gives them to us anyway, because of His amazing grace. We are not anything special, but the Holy Spirit living in us empowers us to live supernaturally.

One day following a live radio broadcast called "Let's Talk About Jesus," I (Dennis) was on my way home. The radio station was next to I-95, which was quite congested that time of day. I remember going down the entrance ramp in my Oldsmobile Cutlass. It had a 350 engine with a four-barrel carburetor. That thing could pass anything but a gas station! I saw my opportunity to merge with the traffic, but just as I noticed the opening I also saw something else! A man in an old beat up Volkswagen was actually passing me on the entrance ramp! Where did he come from? I had to move over or get run over. He took my place in the traffic, but I was able to immediately catch him. To say I was upset would have been the understatement of the year. I had just come from preaching about the love of Jesus, but now I was ready to send this fellow to meet him face to face! I pulled alongside him and asked him what his problem was. He reached down and pulled out a piece of lead pipe, which he promptly swung at my car!

I want to digress here. Earlier that day I had been to the home of a lady in my church. Her husband was having a little struggle with drinking, and an episode involving a gun had recently prompted us to remove the gun from the house. In fact, it was under my seat, going home with me for safe-keeping. I remember reaching down for that big old single-action .45 and thinking, *Buddy, you want to see some lead; I'm fixin'* (that is southern talk for, "I am getting ready to do something") *to show you some lead right now!*

Of course, I did not do it, but what a transition! Within a few minutes after "Let's Talk about Jesus" I was seriously contemplating threatening this guy. Needless to say, condemnation settled in like a cloud. By the time I got home I felt so small I could have walked under the door. Thank God my wife wasn't home. She would have taken one look at my face and wanted to talk about how I was feeling! Moments after my arrival, my self-pity was interrupted by the sound of the telephone. A little voice at the other end of the line said, "Brother De Grasse, I called the radio station and they gave me your number. I heard you today; you are a real man of God." That was like rubbing the salt in my wounds. She then insisted that I pray for her. She told me her whole body was in pain. I remember thinking, "Honey, I will pray for you, but I don't think it will do any good. I don't think God is listening to me right now." After I prayed a perfunctory prayer she loudly exclaimed, "Praise God, the pain is gone." I don't know who was more surprised, she or I.

While I sat there in unbelief I heard the Lord say these words, "It is grace." That is what we believe He is saying to you today. "It is grace." You may have a lot of reasons that make you feel unable to perform. The good news is you do not have to perform. God will perform if you put yourself in His mighty hands for His purposes. We will tell you this: God is not just the God of the second chance; how many chances do you need? He is merciful and patient and desires you to be all that He has called you to be.

Endnote

[1] W.E. Vine, *Vine's Expository Dictionary of Old and New Testament Words* (Old Tappan, NJ: Fleming H. Revell Company, 1981).

Chapter 14

Tune In to God's Frequency

The world in which we live is alive with communication. The very atmosphere is full of telephone conversation, radio shows, television shows, music, movies, news, email, the internet, and who knows what else. It is all there, all you need is the right technology to be able to hear or see it. We are like a radio or television set. When we are tuned in, we can hear from God and we can see things that are beyond the range of normal sight.

On one occasion, a young man who was assisting a prophet found himself in deep trouble. They were trapped by an enemy army that was bent on their destruction. His master, Elisha, did not seem to be troubled at all. He answered, "They that are with us are greater than those who are against us. The servant looked around and saw only the two of them. His master simply said, "Lord, open his eyes and let him see reality." The young man suddenly saw the unseen spiritual realm that existed around them. They were guarded by a host of fiery chariots driven by angelic beings (see 2 Kings 6).

When we are tuned in we can hear from God and we can see things that are beyond the range of normal sight.

Our natural eyes and ears are designed to register certain limited sounds and sights. God can retune them at will to allow us to see and hear what others cannot. He does this to enable us to be more effective in our ministry. We do not have to be limited to what everyone else knows and sees as reality. We live in this earthly dimension, but God lives in all dimensions and can move in all of them at His will. He can enable us to move in His spiritual reality whenever He desires. We call these times "miracles and signs and wonders."

Our radios and televisions have the ability to tune in to the signals that are around us. Our cell phones can receive calls. Our GPS receives signals from a satellite in space and tells us where we are and where we need to go. In the same manner we have been created with the ability to tune in to God. We can turn on our television when we want to watch the news or a sports event. We can turn on our satellite radio if we want to listen to some music. As Spirit-filled Christians, we can tune ourselves into God's channel when we want to. Now, that doesn't mean that we will always hear what we expect to hear or see what we want to see. We just tune in, watch, and pray. If God has anything we need to hear or see, it will become available to us.

We live in this earthly dimension, but God lives in all dimensions and can move in all of them at His will. He can enable us to move in His spiritual reality whenever He desires.

I (Dennis) remember one time I was preparing to go out and preach at a church to which I had been invited. As I sat before the

Lord I felt impressed to pray concerning any particular needs that might be present within the church. As I waited upon God, praying in tongues and listening for "the word of the Lord," I began to perceive different physical needs. I wrote them down on a piece of paper. There were over twenty different maladies and afflictions that came to me. Several days later I was in that church and simply shared the "words of knowledge" with the congregation. People streamed to the front for prayer, and many healings and miracles took place.

It should not surprise us that God would know who would be present and what their particular needs were. It might surprise us what the Lord will share with us. It isn't for us that He does this, but for those who are in need. The more we are willing to work with God, the more He will use us. As I shared those supernatural revelations, the "gift of faith" began to work. People were receiving extra faith to help them receive their miracles and healings. It is fun and easy to work with God. He does most of the work; I like a partner like that!

Hearing the Still, Small Voice of God

How can we tune in to God? The principles are simple, but the application will take a little discipline to accomplish. We live in a society filled with noise and sensory distractions of every sort. For some reason, we are afraid of quietness, especially inner quietness. If we are going to be able to hear the voice of God, we are going to need to practice inner quietness in the secret place; that is where the Lord most often speaks to us. There is a story in the Bible that illustrates this principle. The prophet Elijah was feeling like a failure and hiding out in a cave. At this low point in his life, God visited him with an awe-inspiring revelation of His power and presence in his life.

Then He [God] said, "Go out, and stand on the mountain before the Lord." And behold, the Lord passed by, and a great and strong wind tore into the mountains and broke the rocks in pieces before the Lord, but the Lord was not in the wind; and after the wind an earthquake, but the Lord was not in the earthquake; and after the earthquake a fire, but the Lord was not in the fire; and after the fire a still small voice (1 Kings 19:11-12 NKJV).

Elijah was a man used to hearing "the word of the Lord" or "the inner voice of God" that speaks out of God's Spirit into our spirits and minds. We can learn to listen to that voice. God will never force us to do His will. We can give "the word of the Lord" weight in our lives, or we can diminish it in value. When Elijah heard "the word of the Lord" he immediately responded. God called Elijah out of the cave for a different level of communication. God was going to speak to Elijah audibly. Notice all of the noisy distractions that tested Elijah—a wind so powerful that it broke the rocks, an earthquake, and a roaring fire. God was not in any of those things, but after they passed by, Elijah was able to hear the still, small voice of God.

I (Dennis) know I have heard God's voice this way many times. I was living in Sunrise, Florida, and driving each day to West Palm Beach for my work as a carpet installer. God had been dealing with me about some issues, and on this particular day I heard someone speak to me. It was so real that I turned to see if someone had appeared in my car. The Word of God told me to move back to West Palm Beach and start a church. I obeyed the Lord, but that is another story for another day. There was a lot of testing and trials connected with that decision and I am glad that I heard from God on the matter. When we have heard from God it will help us to endure the testing associated with the will of God. When God moves, there is often a lot of wind, shaking, and fire around. The word of the Lord will help us to endure these things and to enter into His peace.

Bringing Our Thoughts into Submission

Life throws a lot of distractions at us every day. We can learn to bring our thoughts and feelings into submission. We have found that praying in tongues really helps to tune in to the inner voice of the Lord. We also have to put down the other thoughts and distractions that assail us during those times. For example, I (Dennis) often put on some headphones and play some good worship music. Often I like the Celtic versions, to help me to tune in to God. Over the years as I have traveled to many churches, I have practiced sitting in the sanctuary while the worship band practices for the service. I use this time to pray in tongues, wait on God, and get any last minute orders from the Lord. This nourishes my soul and helps me to have the strength and faith to move in God.

There will be times when we will come before the Lord with our own agendas. We may have some burden we need to talk to Him about. There may be some areas of need for which we wish to petition the Lord. We may have to get those things out of the way in order to free ourselves from their demands. If we can discipline ourselves to take the time to press into God, we will be rewarded. It is in those times of listening that He will speak to us. He will make deposits in our spirits that will bring about His will and purposes. Are we saying that every time we do this God will speak to us? No, but if we do not do this we may not hear from Him much, and when and if we do, we may not understand that it is He who is speaking to us.

On one occasion, I (Dennis) had been invited to bring my guitar to a small meeting in order to lead worship. This was after moving back to West Palm Beach and starting the church there. I was invited back for a special meeting, and I remember that the Lord had used me to bring healing to a number of the believers. On the way back home I asked the Lord to explain some things to me. I was curious and my conversation went something like this: "Lord, why is it that sometimes when I go out like this You use me, and sometimes nothing at all happens? Do I just catch You in a good mood, or is it a matter of being in the right place at the right time?"

I do not know if I actually expected to get an answer, but was surprised when "the word of the Lord" came almost immediately, as if God had been waiting for that question.

He said, "What did you do on the way to the meeting?"

Thinking back, I had prayed in tongues for nearly forty-five minutes. I distinctly remember that I said, "Lord, I will do whatever You want me to do, and I am willing to move in a word of knowledge, gift of faith, gifts of healing, prophecy, and whatever else You want to do." I then recalled that sometime during the worship I had stopped and instructed the people, "Let's wait on God and see if He wants to do anything." As we waited, the Lord began to reveal needs to me through "the word of knowledge."

It is important to establish the other part of these miracles and signs and wonders. We actually have to do something with the information we are receiving. We could call this "insider knowledge." It requires some sort of action on our part. As I declared what I was hearing, "the gift of faith" began to operate as well. People began to receive these as words from God for their personal lives. There were several significant healings and some words of encouragement. As I recounted these events, it was as if a light went on in my mind. I understood—it wasn't just God. I had a part in this wonderful event. My part was to "tune in" to the Lord, thereby placing myself at God's disposal by "waiting upon the Lord." This positioned me to hear from Him, see what He wanted done, and then do it.

If all of this seems rather simplistic, you are right. It is simple to work with God. We have made it all so confusing and complicated. He is God; we are not. He does the work, but we are His co-workers. When God wants to get something done He uses His Church. We are the "body" that Jesus has to work with here on the earth. If we are willing to place ourselves at His disposal, He is willing to use us.

Chapter 15

Release What You Have

Peter and John went to the Temple one afternoon to take part in the three o'clock prayer service. As they approached the Temple, a man lame from birth was being carried in. Each day he was put beside the Temple gate, the one called the Beautiful Gate, so he could beg from the people going into the Temple. When he saw Peter and John about to enter, he asked them for some money.

Peter and John looked at him intently, and Peter said, "Look at us!" The lame man looked at them eagerly, expecting some money. But Peter said, "I don't have any silver or gold for you. But I'll give you what I have. In the name of Jesus Christ the Nazarene, get up and walk!"

Then Peter took the lame man by the right hand and helped him up. And as he did, the man's feet and ankles were instantly healed and strengthened. He jumped up, stood on his feet, and began to walk! Then, walking, leaping, and praising God, he went into the Temple with them.

All the people saw him walking and heard him praising God (Acts 3:1-9).

This is an exciting story, and we can learn a lot from this real life account. The first thing we notice is that Peter was well aware of what he did not have—silver or gold. Most of us are aware of our own shortcomings. If we are not aware, it often feels like someone is waiting in the wings to inform us. When the Lord called me (Dennis) to pioneer and pastor a church, I was dumbfounded. I felt so unprepared for that kind of ministry. I knew I could preach, pray for the sick, cast out devils, etc., but this was beyond my experience. One day I asked the Lord, "Are You sure You got the right guy?" When someone would ask all the pastors to stand in a meeting, I would feel like hiding. It took a lot of time for me to reconcile who I thought I was with who God had called me to be. I spent a lot of time looking at what I didn't have, but God wanted me to discover what I had.

Peter had walked with Jesus for several years and had actually experienced the power of God at work. He had gone out in Jesus' name and had seen demons flee. He had witnessed the dead being raised, the lepers being cleansed. Even though Peter knew what he didn't have, he also knew what he did have. In fact, Peter was saying, "I don't have what you expect, but what I do have is so much better, why don't I just give you that instead?"

We often pray wimpy, safety zone prayers. We pray in such a way that if nothing happens, we still look cool!

Notice, Peter and John didn't say, "You are one lucky guy. We are going to prayer meeting right now, and we will submit your name to the prayer chain." In fact, they didn't pray at all. I believe we do not see more miracles because of the methodology of our ministry. We often pray wimpy, safety zone prayers. We pray in such a way that if nothing happens, we still look cool! Peter just released what he had. He prefaced it with "in the name of Jesus." There is nothing magical about that phrase. It is a statement of position and faith. Peter knew what Jesus would do in a situation like this. He had observed Him time and again. Peter was really saying "just as if He were here." What would Jesus do? How would He minister healing? We never see Jesus praying for anyone either. He prayed a lot, but not when it came time to minister. Remember, He did what He saw the Father doing. Peter did what he saw Jesus doing. He reached out his hand and helped this poor man to his feet. The man immediately began to dance his way into the prayer meeting.

Do What Jesus Did

We are convinced that if we want to see Jesus move in our lives like this, we will have to move as Jesus did. We have to do what we see Jesus doing. You may think that Jesus did the miracles because He was God. The Bible is clear on this. While Jesus was on earth He did nothing without the Father. He was not here to show off His power, but to demonstrate the power of the Father. The Bible tells us that He laid aside His godhood and became a servant. He put off His deity and became a man, born of a woman. John said that only a few of the healings and miracles performed by Jesus were recorded. If they had written it all down, John supposed that there wasn't a library large enough to contain the books. We are convinced that God wants to heal, deliver, and raise the dead. He wants to open blind eyes, unstop deaf ears, and cause the mute to speak. He wants the lame to leap and the paralyzed to run.

We do not have to talk God into doing these things. He has clearly demonstrated His desire to bless the sons and daughters of Adam's race. We do need to pray. Jesus often spent the whole night in prayer. He was prepared for whatever the Father would lead

Him into. We can pray too. We can give ourselves over to the will of the Father. We can trust Him as he leads us by the hand. We are not always aware of the leadings of the Father, but as we look back we can clearly see His hand.

We may not always live up to who Jesus was, but He has lived the life for us. His life makes us acceptable to the Father. God sees us in the person of His dear Son. He sees us through the blood of Jesus. You may not feel like you measure up, but Jesus already did measure up, and He gives to you of His own righteousness.

Prepare

How can we release ourselves into the power and ministry of the Lord Jesus Christ? We believe that preparation is important. If you wanted to be a brain surgeon it would take more than you showing up at the hospital and offering your services. There is a lot of training involved. You would begin to head a certain direction in schooling and know that you had a lot of hard work ahead. If you want to take a trip you know that you have to travel in the right direction if you desire to reach your destination. In the same way we must prepare ourselves and set out in the right direction so that we can be released.

Practice

What are we trying to say here? If you feel that God has something for you, what are you doing to prepare yourself? If you feel you are called to preach, are you studying the Word of God and using every opportunity to practice your preaching skills? If you have a burden for the sick, are you taking every opportunity to pray for people? You may not have instant success in your endeavors, but these things are necessary if you are to become successful.

The things you have learned and received and heard and seen in me, practice these things, and the God of peace will be with you (Philippians 4:9 NASB).

Paul is encouraging the believers of his day to "practice." "Practice makes perfect" is an old adage, but a good one. We often expect that we will be like the person who has spent years perfecting his craft. We do not hear about the failures and setbacks he or she has experienced along the way. Failure is often a good teacher. When we get it wrong, the Holy Spirit can teach us the right way. Paul said that we could use his life as an example. God will give us examples along the way. We can pattern ourselves from the good things we have observed in their lives. We should all want others to go way beyond any accomplishments we have made. I am sure that Paul had the same attitude.

I (Dennis) remember our 1959 Ford car. It didn't have power steering like today's cars. It was a beast to steer, until you got it moving. It was an amazing transformation, just a little forward or reverse motion and it got much easier to steer. Many are like that old Ford. They want God to direct them, but they are not willing to actually make any sort of move.

Jump In!

We have observed another method that works in discovering the gifts of the Spirit in our lives—the sink-or-swim method! God has an uncanny way of allowing us to get in over our heads. This will usually encourage us to draw upon His resources. Often as not, others will recognize qualities in us that we do not see. We will get encouraging words from others. Thank God for the Holy Spirit cheerleaders in our lives. Sometimes when we feel as though we are not worth much, someone will come along and share a testimony of how our ministry has blessed them.

God has an uncanny way of allowing us to get in over our heads. This will usually encourage us to draw upon His resources.

Standing on a platform one time, looking over the congregation, I (Dennis) had a vision. Suddenly in my mind I saw a picture of a riverbank. There were people lined up along the bank. They were all dressed for a swim, but the funny part of the picture was the fact that all were wearing life preservers. When God invites us to jump into the deep end of the pool, we need to know that He will be there too. He desires us to succeed. Jesus invited Peter to get out of the boat and to join Him, not *in* the deep, but *on* the deep. Peter stepped out of the boat. Everyone knows Peter began to sink, but the rest of the story is that Jesus did not let him go under! We can do things on our own, but when we are following the guidance of the Holy Spirit, we can be assured that He is with us and will keep us afloat on the sea of life.

Chapter 16

Be Led by the Spirit

My wife, LaVerne, and I (Larry) and a small team of young leaders pioneered a new church in rural Lancaster County, Pennsylvania in 1980 that grew into a church of more than 2,300 within ten years. It was a miracle. I had no seminary training. I had been a chicken farmer in love with Jesus, who just wanted to lead young people to Christ. In 1996, we felt we should decentralize our church into eight local churches in Pennsylvania and start a worldwide church-planting movement. Today, by the grace of God, our family of churches, DOVE Christian Fellowship International (DCFI), spans six continents of the world.

I learned so much during my 15 years serving as a senior pastor. I learned that I needed to focus on my strengths, and find others to resource my weaknesses. I learned it is important to bring in Christian "Holy Spirit specialists" from outside our church to impart to us what we need and share with us what they carry from the Lord. Many years ago, a friend told me about Dennis De Grasse, a former pastor who traveled throughout the world ministering powerfully in prophecy and in the other supernatural gifts of the Holy Spirit. Our church asked Dennis to come for a weekend and we were not disappointed. Dennis ministered among us in integrity and in power. He "read our mail" again and again. He has been used in DCFI, our family of churches, repeatedly for more than 15 years.

I also learned through Dennis and others how important it is to listen to the voice of the Holy Spirit and expect His supernatural gifts to operate through us. For so many of us, our God faithfully and gently leads us and takes us one step at a time.

It was summer camp, and I (Dennis) remember that sometime during the evening an altar call was given and an invitation to receive Christ and to be baptized in water. Suddenly I was surrounded by a presence that blocked out everything else in that room. I found myself out of my seat and walking down that aisle. It was as if everyone else in the room had disappeared, even the noise seemed muted by this overwhelming presence. That was my first experience with the manifest presence of the Holy Spirit. I didn't think about it much at that time—I was only eleven years old—but many years later it made more sense to me.

The Holy Spirit, the third person of the Trinity, is real. The Bible tells us that those who are led by the Spirit of God are the sons of God (see Romans 8:14). That makes it pretty important to try and understand just what this means. We may find ourselves being led by the Holy Spirit and not really be aware that it is happening. Often it is as we look back that we see the hand of God. There are other times when we will be very aware of what He is doing, and we will be able to choose to work with the Holy Spirit.

Here's an experience that might shed some light on the subject. I have a cousin whom I had not seen in a long time and had a great desire to see him, but did not know where he was. I had thought about this several times and mentioned it to the Lord that I would like to see Paul. I knew that he lived somewhere in North Carolina. One day, I left my wife and sons with Jeanne's mom and dad while I went to a church along the South Carolina coast. I had finished my meetings and was heading back to Gatlinburg, Tennessee, where my family was. I had driven this route many times and knew the way without consulting a map. Noticing a sign leading to the interstate via a different road I had never taken, on an impulse I turned down that unfamiliar road. As I approached I-95, I needed to make a stop at the gas station. I remember deliberating whether I would stop here, or wait. I decided to stop.

 We may find ourselves being led by the Holy Spirit and not really be aware that it is happening. Often it is as we look back that we see the hand of God. There are other times when we will be very aware of what He is doing, and we will be able to choose to work with the Holy Spirit.

Having a few miles to drive south on I-95 to pick up I-20 West, as I headed to the interchange of these two interstates I passed several cars. My eyes were drawn to a license plate on the back of one particular car; it was a vanity plate that read "degrasse." Reading that name, I was suddenly aware of my heartbeat. A rush of excitement and adrenalin, much like Christmas morning, flooded my soul. I wondered who this might be. If they were a De Grasse, they were family. Suddenly my turn was before me, and praying that the car would follow me, I slowed and watched my mirror. I was elated to see the vehicle actually turned and was now behind me. Slowing down and lowering my window, I waved my arm and got their attention by blowing my horn several times.

Their car stopped and the passenger window rolled down. A lady looked across the two lanes of highway, as we had stopped on opposite sides of the road. They probably wondered who this kook was! I remember asking them if they were De Grasses and they affirmed they were. I jumped out of the car telling them I was, too. Suddenly my cousin, Paul, got out of the car and approached me. It was a miracle. We went and had a cup of coffee together and caught up on one another's history. He related how he had gotten a late start that day and should have been many miles down the road.

Think of the odds of this meeting taking place without divine intervention. I took a road I had never used before. Paul had gotten up later than planned. We had a window of opportunity that amounted to a few seconds. I call that "being led by the Holy Spirit." Neither Paul nor I had received any verbal communication from the Lord. We just went about our business as usual, but the Lord was at work behind the scenes. He caused our paths to cross in a wonderful way. If anything, this caused my faith to leap to a new dimension. God is able to lead me into His will, even if I am completely unaware of the process. That takes a lot of pressure off me to get it right all the time. God always gets it right.

Will We Trust God's Guidance?

Of course, often the Holy Spirit allows us to know exactly what we need to do. He has the power and ability to communicate His will in such a way that we can see or hear His directions. When the Holy Spirit communicates in this manner, we have to decide what we will do. Will we take a risk and trust the guidance, or will we take a pass? Remember, faith is always a part of these proceedings. We will have to trust the Lord with the outcome. We may need to be willing to lay our lives and our reputations on the altar. God is always looking for those who will obey Him, like David:

"...I have found David the son of Jesse, a man after My heart, who will do all My will" (Acts 13:22 NASB).

The Holy Spirit Is Bigger Than Our Ability to Perceive His Presence

We should make it clear that being led by the Holy Spirit is not the same as being led by compassion or human sympathy. There is nothing wrong with compassion or sympathy, but the Holy Spirit should not be confused with these human emotions. The Holy Spirit is greater than our feelings. He is greater than our sense of God. He is not bound with our human limitations and is able to lift us into the supernatural arena. He may lead us to bless someone that we do not particularly like, or He may lead us to get involved in something that makes us feel uncomfortable and vulnerable.

There have been many occasions when I would simply stand and speak what I saw the Holy Spirit doing, or what I heard Him saying. People testified to being instantly healed, but I did not feel anything at all. On other occasions I have been allowed to experience the power of God flowing through my hands. At times I have sensed the overwhelming presence of God as it surrounded me and then at other times it seemed that God was nowhere around. What does all this mean? It means that the Holy Spirit is bigger than our feelings or our ability or inability to perceive His presence. The Holy Spirit will only witness to the truth and will never witness to a lie. We can trust Him to lead us into all the truth and to reveal the will of God for our lives.

We've all heard people say, "Don't put God in a box." I was talking to the Lord one day about that, and I heard the Holy Spirit reply, "You cannot put God in a box, there isn't one big enough to hold Him. All you do is put yourself in a box." I wonder how many times I have put myself in a box and thereby set limits upon myself. In essence I was saying, "God, You cannot do that through me." When we say that we are like the father of the boy with an evil spirit in the Bible who said, "I do believe, but help me overcome my unbelief" (Mark 9:24). Perhaps that is why the Lord works in stealth mode so often. If we knew too much, we might derail what He desires to accomplish through our lives.

Moving in the Spirit

When I am in a spiritual realm where I sense God's anointing, my faith is at a different level. I am often moving in "the gift of faith." That is a powerful gift in my life. It allows me to believe God for the impossible. I find myself doing things that I would not normally do. While I was in a church in Orangeburg, South Carolina, I heard the Holy Spirit say that He was healing all kinds of joint problems. An older gentleman came forward in response to that word of knowledge. I asked him why he came and he said that his body was stiff all over and he had a lot of pain. He showed me that he could only turn his hand partially. It would not fully rotate as is normal. I began to pray in tongues in the Holy Spirit, and I had the inspiration to command him to turn his hand. I spoke it out in a loud, commanding voice. It just rose up out of my spirit. He turned his hand with the sound of a loud crack. The whole congregation heard it. Being a "great man of faith," my first thought was, "Oh no, he has broken his arm!" I asked him, "Sir, are you OK?"

He responded, "OK? I feel great. I haven't felt this good in years, my whole body feels better." When we are moving in the Spirit of God the impossible becomes commonplace.

Be Willing

The Holy Spirit is ready to lead you today. Your part is to present yourself to Him as a living sacrifice. You need to articulate your desire and your willingness for Him to use you. You will find that He is patient and will teach you how to hear His voice. He will show you how He communicates and He will overlook the times when you fail to recognize His voice. His voice is sometimes subtle. The images He brings into your mind will come quickly and you must be looking for them. If you are inattentive you may miss them completely. You have to purpose in your heart to look and listen for His directions. If nothing comes, that is fine, but often He will share some insider information that will set some person free from pain, confusion, or bondage.

 The Holy Spirit is ready to lead you today. You need to articulate your desire and your willingness for Him to use you.

God Does the Work

God is the one who does the miracles. We are not responsible for the outcome. We cannot heal anyone, but we can prepare ourselves to hear. It is our responsibility to be in the right frame of mind to listen. We have to discipline ourselves to lay our problems down for a season. We have to control our mind and its tendency to wander. We have to bring our emotions under control. We cannot give fear any place in our thoughts as that will short-circuit the whole process. I am not saying that you should never experience any fear, but you have to learn to deal with it. I have learned that if I simply do what the Lord suggests, I am in the anointing, the flow of His spirit, and all fear is forgotten. The "anointing" is that special dispensation of power and ability that God gives us for special purposes.

Are you hungry to see God move? Do you desire to see the lame walk and the blind see? Do you believe that He could use you? Give yourself to Him in a fresh committal to obedience. Ask God to give you a heart that covets the gifts of the Holy Spirit. Learn to be aware of what is going on around and within you. Many of us have heard from God, but have not realized that it was Him. Have you ever had a thought, only to say, "That was just me"? Later on you discovered that it was the Lord and not just your imagination. My prayer for you is this: *May you learn to move in Him. May you be His hands and feet upon this earth, and may you find yourself being His voice in your generation.*

Chapter 17

Break Through the "Saran Wrap" of Fear

*M*y wife would be the first to admit that she is not a morning person. While in college it was even worse due to the late nights studying. She would arise, stumble out of the room to the showers, and try to rouse herself for the day. One morning her friends decided to play a little harmless prank on her. She got up as usual, sleepily gathered her things and opened the door. As she exited the room she was suddenly wrapped in Saran Wrap (a clear plastic wrap to cover food)! To say the least, she was suddenly very awake. I (Dennis) still laugh as the image of that plays in my mind. Even though I was not present I can see it all so clearly. In fact, it sounds like something I might do!

Fear can be like an invisible plastic film that has substance and often surprises us as we exercise the gifts of the Holy Spirit. But we should realize that one step to break through the fear puts us into a dynamic place in God's enabling power. Obviously, we first have to break through. Once in that place where God strengthens us to do things we could never do on our own, we can accomplish the impossible. All of God's resources are put at our disposal, and we can do the will of God. Just as Jesus was anointed for ministry, we, too, can experience His enabling power:

The Spirit of the Lord is upon me, for He has anointed me to bring Good News to the poor. He has sent me to proclaim that captives will be released, that the blind will see, that the oppressed will be set free, and that the time of the Lord's favor has come (Luke 4:18-19).

Remember, God does not ask us to do hard things; He asks us to do impossible things. It is only as we are willing to step out in faith that we will see the impossible happen.

 God does not ask us to do hard things; He asks us to do impossible things.

When I was young in the Lord, and very inexperienced in the things of the Holy Spirit, I found it a little intimidating to allow God to use me. One thing I had going for me was determination. No matter how determined I was I still faced fear each time the Lord called upon me to take a risk. I guess if there was not a little fear it would not be a risk, but I didn't like it.

Each time I felt the urging of the Holy Spirit to speak, pray for someone, prophesy, or whatever, I would feel this barrier of fear rise up before me. I would often pray for it to go away. I would ask the Lord to remove it, but it always seemed to stand firm as a wall before me. The Bible tells us that God has not given us a spirit of fear, but of love and power and a sound mind (see 2 Timothy 1:7). I knew this fear was not from God, but I did not know what to do about it. Although the fear was not enough to make my limbs quake, I would notice my heart rate accelerate, my palms got damp, and my mouth became dry. I also experienced the enemy's voice taunting me, "Who do you think you are? Why would God want to use you?" He would even remind me of some moral fault or failure. It was a real wrestling match. I would tell myself that my sins were forgiven and that God's use of me was His grace. It helps to know what the Scriptures say.

Obey the Holy Spirit's Urgings

Eventually I would have to make a choice. I could either obey the urgings of the Holy Spirit or just ignore them. I noticed that when I chose to obey and step forward to speak for the Lord, the fear would evaporate. I would then find myself in a place where God was obviously present. A great peace would fill my heart and mind and I could see and speak freely for Jesus. This scene would repeat itself again and again over the years. Sometimes it would be the result of accepting an invitation to minister. At first I would be so excited, but then a dread would come upon me. I would promise God that if He would just get me through this message I would never do it again! Of course, that is not what the Lord wanted. He was teaching me His ways. He did not remove the fear because He wanted me to see that it had no power beyond an intimidation factor. In time I began to see that even though it seemed to be perpetually there, it really had no power over me and certainly did not hinder the Lord.

Step on God's Spiritual Snowboard

Fear, whether it is the fear of the unknown, the fear of failure, or the fear of man, has the capacity to paralyze us. The Bible paints a picture of satan as a lion who is roaring out of the darkness. The roar of the lion is meant to paralyze the victim and to give the lion the opportunity to catch a meal. How many times have you been awakened from a sound sleep, only to have your mind become paralyzed by what *might* happen in the future? How many believers have made the choice to just sit in their chair rather than put on their spiritual snowboards and have an adventure with God?

The Holy Spirit will give us a supernatural boldness if we will just be willing to receive it. Peter is a great picture of this truth. He denied the Lord three times the night that Jesus was taken. Peter thought he was a bold man, but fear paralyzed him and he ran into the night, sobbing like a child. After the Holy Spirit baptized him on the day of Pentecost, Peter found a new boldness. He stood before a crowd of hecklers and preached a powerful message that ushered several thousand converts into the Kingdom of God. We have discovered that if we will stand, instead of run, the Holy Spirit will release a boldness in us that will confound the enemy. Satan desired to ridicule the disciples and to beat them down. Peter stood to his feet, lifted his voice, and destroyed the ridicule of the crowd. They couldn't wait to get saved after Peter's anointed message.

 The Holy Spirit will give us a supernatural boldness if we will just be willing to receive it.

I often wondered if that fear would ever go away. After a number of years, I have noticed that it does not have the same power anymore. Once in a while I will still face it, but it virtually has no power over me. Jesus never took it away, but I am glad now that He allowed it to trouble me as the Lord has used it to make me stronger.

What if I'm Wrong?

People often reason, "I would speak out, but what if I am wrong?" We challenge you to think what will happen if you are right! People spend untold fortunes trying to win the big jackpot on the lottery. They stand in line every payday buying those tickets, hoping to strike it rich. You probably have a better chance of being eaten by a polar bear! What are the odds of winning one of those things anyway? We can tell you that you have at least a 50/50 chance of being right with God. It is either Him or it isn't; you win either way. If you are right, you win for being obedient. If you are wrong, the Holy Spirit will teach you to be right the next time.

Some cannot endure the idea of being wrong, reasoning that if they do nothing they will at least not make a mistake. Doing nothing could be the greatest mistake of all. We have found that the odds of being right are actually far greater than 50/50. If we have prayed and taken care of our relationships with God and people, and if we have presented ourselves to the Holy Spirit for His glory, we are in the best place to get it right. Remember, God wants you to succeed. He desires you to learn to be a person capable of being led by the Holy Spirit.

I used to read of the faith of Abraham. The Bible says he was willing to leave everything behind and go somewhere that he had never seen. God considered Abraham's obedience as faith. I always had this thought in the back of my mind that God was going to ask me to do the Abraham thing. He would require me to give up everything that I leaned on for security and just trust Him. It gave me a sense of dread. I had a family and a life. I did not want to do this, but somehow knew it was coming. It may seem mean for God to ask us to give up things for Him, but it is a blessing. You see, when we give these things to Him it releases Him to bless us in turn. That is just what happened. God challenged me to lay it all down for Him. It was not easy because it was not just me. My wife needed to agree as well. My children would have to pay a price too, the absence of their dad from time to time. I have never been sorry that we obeyed God. He has been faithful through the years. I haven't always gotten it right, but that was my own failure, not the Lord's, and He has often rescued me from my follies.

What is it that you are afraid of? What do you dread? Are you afraid of speaking in front of people, of giving your witness to a stranger or your own family? Maybe you are afraid the Lord will call you to prophesy, or teach the Bible, or start a church. Whatever He has for you, there will come a time when you will have to break through the Saran Wrap! Your fear may have substance, but it cannot hold you back. One step of faith and you are on the other side. Just one step and you are in the anointing of the Holy Spirit and you can trust Him with your life and your reputation. Remember, courage is not a lack of fear; courage is doing the right thing in spite of the fear.

Chapter 18

A Time to Pray and a Time to Say

I (Dennis) went to visit an elder in our church. I didn't know that a miracle was about to take place. He had a visitor in his home that was very ill. The man had come to spend the night on a journey and had been there several days as he was too ill to continue his trip. My friend was a little frustrated as they had several small children and the load was getting hard for his wife. I walked into the bedroom and prayed for a few moments in the Spirit. As I prayed, I knew what to do; I simply spoke to him and told him that he was healed and told the sickness to leave him immediately. A look of complete surprise came over him and he declared, "I believe I feel better." He got up and was immediately well. Notice that I did not pray for him in the classical way. I did pray, but that was to see if the Lord would give me any insights in how to minister to him. I just did what I saw in my mind's eye, and he was instantly healed.

I have made it a practice to minister this way since I realized it was how Jesus ministered. I also noticed that the apostles did the same thing. When Peter went in to Tabitha, who was dead, he prayed. I believe he was asking God what should be done. Evidently, he heard from Heaven, for he simply spoke, "Tabitha, arise" (see Acts 9:40 NASB). She was instantly revived and presented alive to the church in Joppa.

Exercise Your Faith!

We see this pattern in the New Testament. Jesus would at times spend the whole night in prayer. Peter prayed for wisdom and grace for the moment's need, but there comes a time when we must exercise our faith and do something. Sometimes speaking, or declaring, is not enough. Remember when Jesus made clay and smeared it on the blind man's eyes? He then sent him to wash it off. When he obeyed he came away healed.

I have seen this work at various times. I remember one incident with a tall, rugged college football player who had extensive damage to his knees. The poor young man could hardly walk. He had come forward because of a word of knowledge. As I ministered to him I felt I should speak to his knees. I simply said, "Knees, you are healed." I then went on to speak to the ligaments, tendons, joints, and connective tissue in those knees telling them they were healed. I asked him if his knees felt any better, and he said no. I went through the process again and got the same results. I knew that God would heal him as He had come via a word of knowledge. Something else needed to be done, and suddenly I commanded him to take a step. He did, but no change was apparent. I then said, "Take another step." This happened several times; suddenly he stated that his knees were feeling better. He was soon running around the room. There were some stairs there and he began to run up and down the stairs. He was totally healed. He needed to do something to receive the healing from God.

Don't Pray Safety Zone Prayers

When we obey the Lord, He takes care of the rest. As I have stated, I am convinced we do not see more happen because we pray safety zone prayers. In other words, we often pray in such a way that we can look cool even if the person is not healed. It is one thing to pray for the Lord to heal people and quite another to tell them they are healed and to get up and walk. I must stress that I am not sharing certain formulas with you. The action taken will depend upon the revelation given. If I do not get any special insight from the Lord, I will just do as I know to do. Many times that is enough to get the job done! I always try to remain open to the revelation of the Holy Spirit.

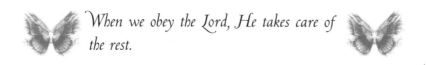

When we obey the Lord, He takes care of the rest.

I have spent a lot of time teaching this information in churches in America and abroad. I have seen the Lord release people to perform miracles in those churches as they prayed and waited on the Lord for instructions. I am convinced that the next major move of God will be a grass roots movement. Jesus desires to move through His Body, the Church, and not just a few special people, but He wants to move through all of us.

God Meets You at Your Point of Expectation

I have found it imperative to determine what people want from the Lord. This was driven home one night in the church at which my father-in-law was the pastor. He is a Spirit-filled Methodist. I guess you could call him a Methacostal! He had invited a couple who were well-known for moving in the healing and miracle ministry. I was the youth leader in the church at that time and was very interested in how they ministered. I remember one woman who had been brought to the meeting who had a withered arm. The couple began to speak to the arm, commanding it to grow out. I was watching that arm grow before my very eyes. Suddenly the woman declared, "That's not what I wanted God to do!" The arm shrank back to its withered state. I remember thinking what a foolish woman she was. She went away with nothing that night.

That event marked me. I realized God will not do what we do not want Him to do. I began to notice that Jesus always asked people what they wanted from Him. He seemed to meet them at their point of expectation. I have made it a practice to ask people what they want. That is a good beginning place. I do this even when people are responding to a particular word of knowledge. When we have established where their faith is, we can then continue to seek the Lord for further wisdom. I have learned to keep my spiritual eyes and ears open. God is apt to show me anything, and I want to be ready to move in that revelation knowledge.

 God will not do what we do not want Him to do.

I was a guest speaker at a church in Florida. God had given me some words of knowledge for different needs. One in particular was for someone with a problem in their lower leg. I remember that no one responded for that word. I went home only to receive a phone call later that afternoon. It was one of the members who hadn't been able to attend the service. In fact, he had his leg in a cast. He had been in a motorcycle accident and the leg was swollen to the point of causing a lot of discomfort. As the brother shared his story, I remember speaking to his leg over the telephone. I commanded the leg to be healed and the swelling to go down. He related that the leg instantly went down and was instantly healed. He was able to remove the cast and walk without any problems. When we move with God, time and space cease to be a factor.

Hear and Obey

Amazing things can happen when we hear the Holy Spirit and then simply obey His directions. I was ministering to some local leaders in Antigua, Guatemala. There was a long line of people waiting to receive ministry. The first person in the line was a young woman. When I inquired of her need the interpreter told me her whole body was in intense pain. I started to pray for her and was just about to release a command for healing when the Holy Spirit checked me. He said, "You might as well not bother to pray, she is in the hands of the tormenter because she is holding a grudge." I asked the interpreter to question her in regards to this revelation, as I did not want to add to her load of grief. She gave affirmation to this word and I then told her that if she would repent and forgive she would be healed. She said she would and was instantly delivered from her pain. Praise God for His faithfulness and mercy.

You may wonder if this is a biblical principle or not. Psalm 107:20 declares that God sent His Word and healed them. When we speak out what we hear from the Holy Spirit, we are speaking His word. God's word is powerful and effective, even when spoken through the lips of an imperfect person. Once again, this presupposes that we have done our homework. These principles work when we are in right relationship with Jesus and with each other. My words have no magical power. It is when I speak the word of the Lord that signs and wonders take place. When we speak the word of the Lord in faith, we are releasing the authority of Jesus into a situation. We are acting as His mouthpiece in this world and His word still has the power to still the raging sea.

There are times when we need to pray and then there are times when we need to act on the revelation we receive from the Spirit of God. It is His desire to set the captives free. He does not willingly afflict His creation. Mercy still smiles in the face of judgment. He will use you, too, if you will but listen and obey.

Chapter 19

Discriminating Between Soul and Spirit

Man is a spirit who has a soul and lives in a body. God gave us a body to allow us to live in the natural universe that He has created. Our body has physical senses that allow us to interact with the world around us. God is a Spirit, and we worship Him in spirit and in truth.

It is the spirit of man that allows him to interact with the Holy Spirit in the realm of God. The spiritual reality is unseen, but is real. Just as we have physical senses, we also have spiritual senses. We can intuitively know and perceive things that are not readily observed by our natural senses alone. Our soul is the part of us that allows these two very different realities, these two different kinds of senses, to come together. It is the spirit of man that allows him to know God and to fellowship with Him. In fact, as the Scripture tells us, the natural man cannot know God.

"No eye has seen, no ear has heard, and no mind has imagined what God has prepared for those who love Him."

But it was to us that God revealed these things by His Spirit. For His Spirit searches out everything and shows us God's deep secrets. No one can know a person's thoughts except that person's own spirit, and no one can know God's thoughts except God's own Spirit. And we have received God's Spirit (not the world's spirit), so we can know the wonderful things God has freely given us.

When we tell you these things, we do not use words that come from human wisdom. Instead, we speak words given to us by the Spirit, using the Spirit's words to explain spiritual truths. But people who aren't spiritual can't receive these truths from God's Spirit. It all sounds foolish to them and they can't understand it, for only those who are spiritual can understand what the Spirit means (1 Corinthians 2:9-14).

The natural man is one who is unregenerate or not born again. The natural man only perceives with his natural senses and has access to his own thoughts to guide him. The spiritual man receives information from the spiritual realm as well, and the Holy Spirit helps him to interpret these things.

Man was created to have fellowship with God. It follows that God has created within the spirit of man the capacity to do so. When a child is born, if it is normal, it will go through a learning process. It will learn to live and operate the senses within its body. Who can forget the first word our precious child spoke, or the first step they took? We start out as helpless infants, but eventually, if all goes well, we learn to take care of ourselves.

Learning to Walk in the Spirit

The spiritual part of our lives is no different. There are laws that govern the spiritual as well as the natural creation. When learning to walk in the natural, we must deal with the law of gravity. We learn balance and control of our muscles. In the spirit we must learn to walk, too. Because we do not know anything about the realm of the spirit, it is easy for us to become confused, lose our balance and take a tumble. Of course, there are unseen forces that are always trying to trip us up as well. If we believe in God we will have to accept the fact that satan and his hoard of evil demons are real, too. Some have forgotten this and have wandered off into the darkness. Some have embraced the reality of this spiritual dimension, but have rejected the reality of their lost conditions. They have chosen to reject the idea of God, or they have embraced some idea like "The Force." They see no need for a savior, they do not believe in Heaven or hell, and they are unaware of the malevolent nature of the demonic forces. They reject the reality of a personal devil. Some have had contact with these beings and see them as benevolent beings, those who have passed over before us. These beings claim to be spiritual guides, looking out for our spiritual welfare, but they are very practiced at seduction and deception. Their whole purpose is to destroy as many humans as possible.

The Realm of the Spirit

You may wonder why we are talking like this. It is because the realm of the spirit can be a dangerous place. Do you remember when you first got your driver's license? Were your parents a little nervous to let you take the car out the first time? How about when you watched your own child drive out of sight for the very first time? We know all the things that can happen out there, and we are rightly concerned, but driving is a fact of life, a calculated and necessary risk. If we are informed of the possible and very real dangers, and if we have learned to observe the laws of the road, chances are we will be all right. We need to approach this walk in the Spirit of God the same way.

Several years ago a small child was killed. He had stumbled upon a nest of baby rattlesnakes. They were cute and he was young and inexperienced. He handled them and was consequently bitten many times, and he died as a result. Satan knows how to take advantage of our ignorance, our sense of immortality, our pride, and our arrogance. He knows how to make something deadly appear to be harmless or beneficial. Remember his tactics with Eve? What we are saying is: be humble and teachable. Allow the Holy Spirit to guide you in the realm of the Spirit. He will send teachers your way who will mentor you. He will also arrange life lessons that are custom made for you. Listen to Him, learn the lessons, and you will prosper; ignore Him at your own peril.

  Allow the Holy Spirit to guide you in the realm of the Spirit. He will arrange life lessons that are custom made for you.

Our heart relationship with God is the most important protection we can have. We also need to feed on the Word of God and understand the streams of truth that run through its pages. We must maintain relationships with others God has given to us. They have the right to speak into our lives. God has placed spiritual authority over us for a reason. He wants us to be safe from satan's plans and schemes.

The Phenomenon of God's Presence

When God manifests His presence in a place, we may experience some strange phenomenon. We may feel goose bumps, great senses of joy, spiritual intoxication, or even pass out from His overwhelming presence. These can be exciting experiences, and they can be addictive, but we need to guard against the temptation to confuse these manifestations as God. When God came to the prophet Elijah there was a strong wind, an earthquake, and fire. None of these things were the Lord, but it would be easy to give them more emphasis than they deserve. We want to feel God and experience Him. There is nothing wrong with these desires, but if we do not understand human nature we may set ourselves up for some deception. God is not a feeling or a wind. He is more than goose bumps, or a feeling of peace. All of these experiences, and more, may appear at His presence, but their lack does not mean that He is not around.

Most of us have experienced these very sensations under very different circumstances. Have you noticed the rush of emotion that comes when someone sings your National Anthem? Is that the Holy Spirit, or just our emotions? It isn't the presence of God, but it can feel the same. Our soul manifests these different feelings. We can see people get inspired at a pep rally to the point of great exuberance. We have seen the same thing during times of praise and worship. While this is not wrong, we need to be careful that we do not confuse an emotional or physical response as God Himself. You may think that we are getting too picky, but even though the difference is subtle it is important that we understand.

I (Dennis) used to lead a group of young adults. One in the group loved to go into the sanctuary, turn off all the lights except the blue light that outlined the cross, and then we would all hold hands in a circle and pray. Somehow this helped her to make a connection with God. It did not seem right to her without that light. K-Mart used the same tactics for years to get people to buy things—it was called "the blue light special!" I like to play soft music, preferably of the Celtic origin, while I pray and study. These things are not necessarily wrong, but what if I do not have access to the music, or what if the blue light is burned out? We must take care to seek God, not the feeling we had when the blue light was on.

When we move in the Spirit, we may not have any of those sensations. It may be an act of faith, or an act of our willingness to simply obey God. Those props are nice, and God may allow us to enjoy them for a season, but He may wean us from them and teach us to stand in faith. Feelings are like training wheels on a bicycle. When my son was young, he was determined to ride a two-wheeler that had been given to him as a gift. We lived on a circle so he had plenty of room to practice. That boy looked like he had been in a war zone. He was scraped from head to toe! I felt so guilty that I went and spent money that I couldn't afford to buy him a set of training wheels. He would ride around and around that circle, bouncing from side to side. Those training wheels did the trick. One day I noticed that the side to side motion of his cycling style had caused those wheels to elevate themselves a couple of inches. They no longer touched the ground, they were on the bike, but he did not need them anymore.

God will allow us training wheels for a while, but will eventually expect us to mature enough that we can operate without them. Faith is more than a feeling. I have seen great miracles happen with absolutely no feelings at all. My trust is in God and in His word. When He tells me He is going to do something, I am going to believe Him. I will stake my life on His faithfulness.

My wife once asked me the difference between prophecy and fortune telling. I told her that fortune telling was the counterfeit. In order to have a counterfeit, there must be a real. Clairvoyance, spirit reading and writing, mental telepathy, contacting the dead, all of these things are the devil's counterfeits. Satan has limited power and he can grant a person power to accomplish what may look like miracles, but when the devil does a miracle, it is to bring a soul into captivity and their eventual destruction. Apparently, satan has access to certain knowledge. He will share his knowledge in order to condemn someone to hell. The gifts of darkness are designed to bring a person into more and more darkness and bondage, but the gifts of the Holy Spirit will set the captive free!

Have you ever had someone preach at you while he prayed over you? You heard every complaint, everything that you needed to change lifted up in the form of a prayer. Some have used prophecy in the same way. They express their own thoughts, fears, and complaints prefaced by a "thus says the Lord." We can counsel people out of our own perceptions and agendas. In the same way, we may be guilty of forwarding our own thoughts, plans, and agendas as though they were received as revelation from God.

 The gifts of darkness are designed to bring a person into more and more darkness and bondage, but the gifts of the Holy Spirit will set the captive free!

I do not like to know a lot about people before I minister to them. I do not want any information coloring my spiritual perceptions. If I do know something in the natural, I am always careful to give a disclaimer, such as, "I know this in the natural, but this is what I feel God is saying…" I might even say, "This is just my own opinion." I do not want my ideas to sound like they are God's word on the matter. I do not want to create the false idea that God revealed something to me, when all the time it was someone else who let it slip. I want people to put their faith in the word of God, not the word of Dennis. Even in healing I may know of a need. I will say, "I know this in the natural, but I believe God wants to do something here." I have seen God heal in this way too. Just be real and honest with people.

In the Old Testament, the false prophets were prophesying out of their own spirits. They were speaking out what they believed or wanted to happen, rather than speaking for God. If I am going to speak for God I may not be politically correct at times. I may speak into a situation to bring correction. If I know what is going on in a situation, I will take a pass and not prophesy into it. I might give my opinion, but will refrain from giving it a divine appearance. I usually do not prophesy into the lives of those who are close to me. I know too much about them. I have too many opinions of my own regarding their lives. I am free to speak in other ways, but will not pretend that it is the "word of the Lord."

People need to know that we are credible witnesses for God. They need to know that we are not politically or selfishly motivated. They need to see that we are not trying to promote our own ministries, but are promoting the word of the Lord. As we follow God in the Spirit, He will promote us at the right time and in the right way. God will honor us as we honor Him.

Chapter 20

Things We Have Witnessed

We were on a six-week, five thousand mile tour with a group of about eighteen others. They were mostly teenagers, the pastor and his wife, and a few young adults. Jeannie and I (Dennis) were along as part of the team. We were in Baton Rouge, Louisiana, and had spent some time ministering there along with the team. We were singing and testifying for Jesus. After the meeting a brother came up to me and asked why I walked with a limp. Others had asked me about this, but I was not conscious of it. I guess I had done it for so long, I did not notice it. He sat me down in a pew, lifted my legs and just held them underneath the heel. I noticed that one leg was notably shorter, and as he began to pray I felt a stretching sensation in that leg, as though it were made of rubber! The leg immediately grew out so that they were both the same length. I am grateful that God didn't just shrink the long one! The limping ceased and something was released into my life at that time.

A few weeks later we were home. I was working for my father-in-law as his youth pastor. After returning, I shared all the things that we had witnessed on our ministry trip. I didn't know it, but God had set the stage for a move of the Holy Spirit in our midst. We began to pray for miracles, and the Lord began to move. One girl had a leg that was over two inches shorter in length. She sat down in a pew and we prayed for her. It was amazing! Her leg shot out! She testified to having to let the hem down in all of her pants. Several others had the same needs. Needless to say, faith was ignited in the hearts of those teens. One young lady was severely bow legged. She wondered if the Lord could straighten her legs. We simply held up her legs by her heels and watched them straighten before our very eyes. The youth were never the same after that. One of those young men became a deacon in our first church plant.

In the first chapter of Acts, Luke states that he had testified, in the book of Luke, about all that Jesus had taught and done. Jesus did not just teach the Word, He performed many miracles and signs and wonders. That is the gospel way. God is more than willing to do the same today. When people see the works of God, it does something in their faith. Something is released in their lives, and they will never be the same again.

It is God who heals, saves, and delivers, but He uses us to do it. I remember a sister in Christ who came to me in a service in the Liverpool area of England. She was in tears and shared that while I was ministering to other people a tumor had just disappeared from her body. She said that it was as big as a grapefruit and it had just vanished. Does that sound impossible to you? Without God it could be taken out of her flesh by cutting it out, but God just removed it by His power. I hope that if I ever need any surgery it will be done that way.

 It is God who heals, saves, and delivers, but He uses us to do it.

Some of the most exciting things I have witnessed have been when believers have stepped up to the plate and had a turn at bat.

I often teach on releasing healing and miracles with an end to release and activate the believers. I usually call all who need healing forward. I then ask for volunteers to come and stand with them. I then get the candidates for healing to share their expectations with the volunteers. After some instruction I release the people to minister. It is amazing the testimonies that come from those times. Healings, miracles, and signs and wonders are common when we are willing to simply step out in faith.

One evening I was sharing these principles with our home church in North Carolina. I called the sick forward and then got the volunteers forward to minister. One Christian sister ended up on the floor. She had a number of issues, one of which was scoliosis. She told me later that as she lay upon the floor, she felt someone pulling on her legs. She looked to find no one there. She was also pregnant which aggravated her condition greatly. She felt as though something had changed in her body and asked her husband to verify her suspicions, which he did. God had straightened her back and she was delivered from the pain she normally had. Later that evening she was lying on the couch and noticed something else. She had been born with flat feet, as she looked at her feet she saw that they had arches! God had not only healed her spine, He had given her arches in her feet as well. Jesus, You're just too much!

I was ministering in a church in South Carolina. We had prayed for the sick and afflicted and many had received some immediate relief. The meeting was over and we were packing up to go when a young woman came to me asking for ministry. She had had surgery several years before. They had surgically removed a joint from one of her toes and for five years she had to walk on the side of that foot. I cannot imagine how uncomfortable that must have been. I asked her if she believed that God could heal it and she affirmed that she did. I remember simply speaking, "Toe, you are healed. I command a new joint to form in you right now!" I then told her to take a step, which she did. Her toe was instantly healed and she was able to walk normally. I saw her a year later and she smiled and said, "Look, I am wearing high heels." What a God we serve! When we are moving in faith and in the Holy Spirit anything can happen!

It pays to keep your spiritual eyes open. I was in a church in North Florida where I was the guest minister. I was praying, "Lord show me what You are doing here today," as I was looking up on the platform. I closed my eyes to shut myself into the secret place with the Lord. When I closed my eyes I could see the outline of the platform and the pulpit that was on it. I had been staring at it while praying and my mind had imprinted the image, but I was seeing something else as well. Standing next to the pulpit was a tall man. He looked to be about seven or eight feet in height. I opened my eyes to see and there was no one by the pulpit at all. As soon as I closed my eyes, there he was again and I could see that he was holding out a sword. I also noticed that a line was drawn that separated the church, neatly dividing it in two. I have to say that I jumped to conclusions and thought, "Poor pastor, he has a split in his church." I am glad that I had the presence of mind to keep that to myself and just pray over what I was seeing.

It is easy to jump to conclusions if we are not careful. I had seen something and my mind had interpreted what I saw, but I was not comfortable with my conclusions. I then began to pray, "Lord, what are You showing me?" I needed some advice from the Holy Spirit! As I waited on the Lord and prayed in the Spirit, I heard these words come into my mind. "There are a lot of sick people here today, if they will get up, form a line, and march around the church, I will heal them when they cross that line."

My next thought was, "Lord, I am not Benny Hinn; I am just plain vanilla; I do not minister that way."

The Holy Spirit said, "You asked Me and I told you; it is up to you." Needless to say, when my time for ministry came I shared that vision and those words. About three fourths of the church stood to their feet and made a line. As they marched around God began healing them. Most testified to receiving immediate relief that morning.

Jesus said, "Of My own Self, I am not able to do anything. I do what I see the Father doing and I speak what I hear the Father saying." That is a De Grasse paraphrase, but it is accurate. I am learning to minister that way as well. It sure takes a lot of strain out of ministry. My part is to prepare myself by ministering to the Lord and then to simply make myself available for His will. He does all the real work!

While ministering in North Florida and praying for a woman, I saw a picture of a huge angel standing behind her, covering her with his wings. I did not know what that meant, but as I simply shared what I saw, she began to weep. Later I heard her story. She and her husband, who was recently deceased, were part of a church that was a little controlling to say the least. Her husband had died unexpectedly as a young man and had left her bereft of money. He had left a business, no insurance—you get the picture. She had decided to move on to another church, but the leaders had warned her that she would not have the proper spiritual covering if she left. They warned her that she would be vulnerable and out of the will of God for her life. That simple vision had ministered to her. God was assuring her, "I have got you covered!"

I was standing in the congregation of a church in Texas. I was stationed at Fort Sam Houston, going through my basic and advanced training to become a medical corpsman. I was helping to lead some worship in this church and was enjoying the ministry of a couple who had just come from Mexico. They owned their own bakery and raised their own money to support their ministry. They were relating the miracles and healings they had observed. The woman stopped her speaking, looked directly at me and said, "Young man, you are going to have signs and wonders following your ministry." I felt that word enter into my spirit. There were many times that I hung onto that word for dear life. I kept reminding myself that there were better days ahead. I would tell myself that the Lord was not through with me as there were still unfulfilled promises. Prophetic words can encourage us and give us the strength to go on when we really want to quit.

 We need these gifts in operation if we are going to have strong and healthy families, church families, and ministries.

Generally speaking, the heart of God is to encourage the Church and to build up the believers. We need these gifts in operation if we are going to have strong and healthy families, church families, and ministries. We may be in the midst of a terrible tragedy, we may have suffered the worse kind of loss, but one word from God can change everything. If we are willing, the Lord may use us to deliver that word or to release that miracle for some needy soul.

Chapter 21

God Wants to Use You

It was a rainy Sunday morning and, as usual, our church parking lot was a soggy mess. Living in Delaware put the ground water level about six inches below the surface of the ground; at least it seemed that way whenever we had much precipitation! We needed a real parking lot; the ladies were ruining their shoes and the mud being tracked into the building was becoming a real chore to clean up. We had investigated the cost of a real parking lot; it would cost about ten thousand dollars to see it done. It might as well have been a million! But that day as I (Dennis) stood at the front of the church as the congregation made their way to their seats I declared, "God will give us a parking lot!" I had a real sense of confidence about this and I declared it several times over the next few months, in fact, every time it rained.

One day I arrived at the church office to get the news from my associate: "We are getting a parking lot!" I asked for the details and found out that a local construction company had come by and declared the Lord had told them to give us a parking lot. They came with their heavy equipment, mucked out tons of topsoil, graded, and hauled in tons of stone—all free of charge to us. The only portion we had to pay for was the paved entrance to the road. We had the funds to do that. It was an amazing gesture of generosity on their part, and they later told us that God had richly rewarded their obedience. The owner of the company testified that when they went to the next job, God gave him an idea. God showed him how to do the job a different way. They made so much unexpected profit on that job that they were set for the rest of the year. God is amazing!

Declare What You Have Heard from the Lord

One day the Lord spoke to the prophet Elijah. God was dealing with the ungodly government of Ahab and Jezebel. Through the prophet, God had called for a drought to come upon the land. Several years later, the Lord decided that it was time to bring His judgment out into the open and confront the idolatry that was so prevalent in Israel (see 1 Kings 18:1). The Lord told Elijah to go and present himself to Ahab, for the Lord declared that He would send rain upon the earth. As we follow this story, we see Elijah ascending to the top of Mt. Carmel to pray. He knelt down on the earth and began to pray for rain. There is something interesting here. First of all, Elijah was not praying his own desires here. Elijah was declaring what he had heard from the Lord. Here is the sequence of events. Elijah prayed until he heard from God, then Elijah prayed what he heard, until what he heard was what he saw. He stayed on his knees, declaring what he had heard from Heaven, while his servant informed him of the progress. Soon the servant reported the appearance of a cloud, about the size of a man's hand. That might not have seemed much to anyone else, but to Elijah it was enough. He recognized what was happening and said, "Better run for cover, we are going to have a gully washer for sure!" When we are moving in the purpose of God, we will often recognize the signs of the times. We will often have a sense of what is happening and why.

Use Your Spiritual Eyes

God wants us to be men and women like Elijah—people who will minister to God and who will be listening for the word of the Lord. Believers who will boldly declare what they have heard and who will act out of what they have seen through the eyes of faith. Abraham saw Jesus' day and rejoiced in what he saw, but that was several thousand years before it happened in our realm. Our spiritual eyes can transcend time and space. We can see and hear things that others cannot. As we pray into those things and begin to declare them, we are acting as God's agents here on earth. We have a durable power of attorney in Jesus Christ our Lord. It is our right and privilege to represent God here on the earth. He gives us authority and power to do these things in Jesus' name. It is the Holy Spirit who leads us and guides us into the will of the Lord for our lives and ministry. He is the one who takes the Word of God and makes it alive.

 It is our right and privilege to represent God here on the earth.

We want to make it clear that this is not just positive thinking or mind over matter. This is not just something *you* would like to see happen. This initiative is not political or social, but is born out of the heart of God Himself. He is the great initiator and He wants you to be on His team. He wants you to open your hearts and minds to all the possibilities that are in the Kingdom of God. God doesn't need our ideas; He has plenty of His own. God doesn't need our strength or our talents; He needs our cooperation and our obedience.

For a season, I (Dennis) lived in North Florida. During that time, there was a rather large fire burning in South Georgia, about sixty miles away from our home. The fire was burning in a swamp and the smoke was terrible. We had been having a rather severe drought in the area and needed rain badly. I remember sharing the truth of intercession with the local church and had challenged the body to begin to intervene for rain. I believed that God had told me that if the church would stand in the gap, He would move. God told me to practice what I had been preaching, so I went outside and spoke to the heavens. I began to tell the winds to bring rain to our area and the sky to release the moisture upon our land to put out the fire.

Within a few days, an unseasonable tropical storm formed off the coast near Jacksonville, Florida. It seemed like an answer to my intercessions. I was disappointed when it petered out and barely rained at all along the coast. I asked the Lord what was happening. A day or so later, while listening to the weather, I heard the forecaster stating that a high-pressure system was responsible for keeping the rain out. It had parked over the entire Southeast as a stationary high-pressure ridge. I had the answer I needed and began to command that system to move out of the area and to allow the rain to come. Within two days rain came and put out the fires burning in the Okefenokee Swamp.

Once again, I am sure others were praying as well, but I am sharing what happened in my life. When we listen to the Holy Spirit and obey His directives, I believe we can make a difference. I do believe that one person can make a difference when they are in partnership with God. We sometimes think the more we get involved the better it will be. Maybe our prayers can tip the scales in our favor, but I believe when we do what the Lord commands, He will tip the scales Himself. He is looking for those who will partner with Him. There are many situations taking place in our lives, our families, and our nation that need God's involvement, but our partnership is often the key to His intervention.

In Training for Reigning!

We are well aware that the whole area of the supernatural power of God and the gifts of the Holy Spirit has been controversial in the church in the western world. But in the early church and in most of the nations that we travel to, the demonstration of the power of God was and is a reality. Paul the apostle said:

> *And my message and my preaching were very plain. Rather than using clever and persuasive speeches, I relied only on the power of the Holy Spirit. I did this so you would trust not in human wisdom but in the power of God* (1 Corinthians 2:4-5).

God can use angels to fulfill His will on the earth, and at times He does, but He has chosen to use His children. We are imperfect, plagued with all kinds of faults and failures, and sometimes we have a hard time hearing, seeing, or believing, but the Lord is patient. The Holy Spirit will send teachers into our lives. He will also use life experiences to instruct us. We are in training for reigning after all!

You Can Do Even Greater Works

Remember, since Jesus did what He did because He was the Son of Man and used the Holy Spirit to do it, you can do it also. Jesus was directed by the Holy Spirit, just as you are. You can have the same kind of ministry because you have the same Holy Spirit that He had. It's hard to believe, but we can do the same works that Jesus did! Jesus Himself said in John 14:12, "...anyone who believes in Me will do the same works I have done, and even greater works, because I am going to be with the Father."

God wants us to expect great things. In the 1970s, in Ludwigsburg, Germany, there was a place called Canaan Land. It was a wonderful Christian community that had been literally raised from the rubble of World War II. God had spoken to a German Christian woman to go there and build a center for a witness and for healing. The city nearby had been nearly destroyed and the land they purchased was a desert. They hired a geologist to find water and were told that there was no water. God told the sisters to dig a lake in faith. When they completed the task and drilled, it filled with water. In fact, they had so much water that they could supply the nearby city. If we are willing to take a risk for the glory of God and will simply obey Him, we will see the goodness of the Lord.

There Are No Expiration Dates on Your Prayers

Our intercessions, prayers, and declarations have no shelf life. Many of us are walking in the things of God because someone interceded for us. It may have been someone several generations in our past that was moved upon by the Spirit of God to intercede for our lives. We may not be able to visit the nations of the earth, but we can stand in the gap for them. Our prayers, intercessions, and declarations will cross every boundary and barrier erected by man or devil. As we pray we may hear ourselves saying some things that will surprise us. We may be surprised at the boldness and the confidence of our words, but remember, God watches over His words to perform them (see Jeremiah 1:12).

 Our intercessions, prayers, and declarations have no shelf life.

Our prayer for you is that you will be encouraged to make yourself available to the Most High God. It is up to Him what kind of adventures you will have, but understand this: you will have adventures of the highest kind. We have been given the privilege to be in a partnership with God Himself and He has given to us His Holy Spirit as a seal and a pledge of what is to come. In this day and hour the Lord is calling His Church to arise in faith, power, and obedience to fulfill its ministry and destiny. If you can hear that call, then be as Samuel of old and say "Lord, here am I, your servant is listening."

Get Started

Jesus functioned with the same nine supernatural spiritual gifts in the New Testament that are available to us, so we can do the same. We have the same Holy Spirit that He had when He walked on this earth. Start where you are at. Before you try to trust God to see someone raised from the dead, you might want to trust Him to heal a backache. Just get started. Like the disciples learned from Jesus, you too can learn from others. Surround yourself with those who are mature in the operation of the gifts so you can grow in them. The last chapter of the book of Acts is still being written. It is now your turn to be a vital part of experiencing the Kingdom of God being manifested on earth as you walk in the supernatural gifts of the Holy Spirit. "God has given each of you a gift from His great variety of spiritual gifts. Use them well to serve one another" (1 Peter 4:10). Just be real and expect our God to use you to minister to others in the power of the Holy Spirit in a supernaturally natural way!

Appendix

Seven Steps to Being Filled With the Holy Spirit

1. We must realize that every believer has the Holy Spirit living in them (see Rom. 8:9; 1 Cor. 3:16).

2. We need to recognize the difference between having the Holy Spirit living in us and being filled with the Holy Spirit (see John 20:22; Acts 2:1-4).

3. Being filled with the Holy Spirit gives us spiritual power (see Acts 1:8). The most common scriptural manifestations of the initial evidence of being filled with the Holy Spirit are prophesying (proclaiming the truth) and speaking in tongues (speaking in a heavenly language) (see Acts chapters 2, 4, 8, 9, 10, 19 and 1 Cor. 14:14-15).

4. God gives the Holy Spirit to those who ask Him (see Gal. 3:14). If earthly fathers give good gifts to their children, how much more will our heavenly Father give the Holy Spirit to those who ask Him (see Luke 11:11-13).

5. Many times, people in the Bible received the Holy Spirit through the laying on of hands (see Acts 9:17 and Acts 19:1-7).

6. When we receive the baptism in the Holy Spirit, we receive this gift with the understanding that nine spiritual gifts are contained within this one gift (see 1 Cor. 12:7-10). God will teach us how to use each of these individual gifts.

7. We need to be filled with the Holy Spirit again and again (see Acts 4:31; Eph. 5:18). We have a tendency to leak!

Other Books by Larry Kreider

Building Your Personal House of Prayer

Authentic Spiritual Mentoring

Speak Lord, I'm Listening

Starting a House Church

The Biblical Role of Elders in Today's Church

Hearing God 30 Different Ways

The Cry for Spiritual Fathers & Mothers

Resources from DCFI

Building Your Personal House of Prayer by Larry Kreider

If you love to pray, or you need to pray more effectively, this book will change your prayer life forever. Your entire approach to prayer is about to improve! Imagine eagerly awaiting your prayer time, praying with confidence, and having your heart full of faith as you commune with God. This book is a gold mine of tools you need to have the prayer life you know you want and need! 254 pages: $15.99 ISBN: 978-0-7684-2662-5

Speak Lord! I'm Listening by Larry Kreider

Jesus said, "My sheep hear my voice," but many Christians do not know how to hear from God. In this practical, story-rich guidebook, international teacher Larry Kreider shows believers how to develop a listening relationship with the Lord. It explores the multiple ways Christians can hear the voice of God in today's world, offering real-life examples—not theory—of how God teaches His followers to listen, with tips in each chapter for distinguishing His voice from the noise of satan's interference. Christians across the denominational spectrum will develop a closer and deeper relationship with God as they learn 50 unique ways to listen to Him. You will realize that God was speaking to you all along but, like the disciples on the road to Emmaus, you didn't know it was Him! 224 pages: $14.99 ISBN: 978-0-830746-12-5

Hearing God 30 Different Ways by Larry Kreider

The Lord speaks to us in ways we often miss, including through the Bible, prayer, circumstances, spiritual gifts, conviction, His character, His peace, and even in times of silence. Take 30 days and discover how God's voice can become familiar to you as you develop a loving relationship with Him. 224 pages: $14.99: ISBN: 978-1-886973-76-3

The Cry for Spiritual Fathers & Mothers by Larry Kreider

Returning to the biblical truth of spiritual parenting so believers are not left fatherless and disconnected. How loving, seasoned spiritual fathers and mothers help spiritual children reach their potential. 186 pages: $12.99: ISBN: 978-1-886973-42-8

The Biblical Role of Elders for Today's Church by Larry Kreider, Ron Myer, Steve Prokopchak, and Brian Sauder

New Testament principles for equipping church leadership teams: Why leadership is needed, what their qualifications and responsibilities are, how they should be chosen, how elders function as spiritual fathers and mothers, how they are to make decisions, resolve conflicts, and more. 274 pages: $12.99: ISBN: 978-1-886973-62-6

Biblical Foundations for Your Life:

This two-book series by Larry Kreider covers basic Christian doctrine. Practical illustrations accompany the easy-to-understand format. Use for small group teachings (48 in all), a mentoring relationship, or daily devotional.

Also Available in Spanish!

Biblical Foundations for Your Life: Discovering the Basic Truths of Christianity by Larry Kreider. 310 pages: $17.99: ISBN: 978-0-7684-2748-6

Biblical Foundations for Your Life: Building Your Life on the Basic Truths of Christianity by Larry Kreider. 306 pages: $17.99: ISBN: 978-0-7684-2749-3

Authentic Spiritual Mentoring by Larry Kreider

In this book, Larry Kreider offers proven biblical keys that will open the door to thriving mentoring relationships. You will learn the Jesus Model of mentoring—initiate, build and release—and how to apply it to the spiritual family God is preparing for you. Whether you are looking for a spiritual mentor or desiring to become one, this book is for you! 224 pages. ISBN:978-0-8307-4413-8

Growing the Fruit of the Spirit by Larry Kreider and Sam Smucker

This book encourages you to take a spiritual health check of your life to see if you are producing the Bible's nine exercises for spiritual wellness as mentioned in Galatians 5:22-23 and expressed in the believer as growing the fruit of the Spirit. 160 pages: $14.99: ISBN:978-1-886973-93-0

Helping You Build Cell Churches Manual compiled by Brian Sauder and Larry Kreider

A complete biblical blueprint for small groups, this manual covers 51 topics! Includes study and discussion questions. Use for training small group leaders or personal study. 224 pages: $19.95: ISBN: 978-1-886973-38-1

Church Planting and Leadership Training

(Live or video school with Larry Kreider and others)

Prepare now for a lifetime of ministry and service to others. The purpose of this school is to train the leaders our world is desperately looking for. We provide practical information as well as Holy

Spirit empowered impartation and activation. Be transformed and prepared for a lifetime of ministry and service to others.

If you know where you are called to serve…church, small group, business, public service, marketplace or simply want to grow in your leadership ability—our goal is to help you build a biblical foundation to be led by the Holy Spirit and pursue your God-given dreams. For a complete list of classes and venues, visit www.dcfi.org.

School of Global Transformation (seven-month residential, discipleship school)

Be equipped for a lifetime of service in the church, marketplace and beyond! The School of Global Transformation is a seven month, residential, discipleship school that runs September through March. Take seven months to satisfy your hunger for more of God. Experience His love in a deeper way than you ever dreamed possible. He has a distinctive plan and purpose for your life. We are committed to helping students discover destiny in Him and prepare them to transform the world around them.

For details, visit **www.dcfi.org.**

Seminars

One Day Seminars with Larry Kreider and other DOVE Christian Fellowship International authors and leaders:

Building Your Personal House of Prayer

How to Fulfill Your Calling as a Spiritual Father/Mother

How to Build Healthy Leadership Teams

How to Hear God—30 Different Ways

Called Together Couple Mentoring

*How to Build Small Groups—Basics for Healthy cell Ministry
Helping you develop strategy for successful cell groups*

How to Grow Small Groups—Advanced

Counseling Basics

Effective Fivefold Ministry Made Practical

Starting House Churches

*Planting Churches Made Practical: Fulfill your calling
to plant a church and fulfill the Great Commission*

How to Live in Kingdom Prosperity

How to Equip and Release Prophetic Ministry

For more information about DCFI seminars,
call: 800-848-5892 or e-mail: seminars@dcfi.org.

Resources from Dennis De Grasse

Gifts of the Holy Spirit Seminars

These seminars are designed to not only introduce the gifts of the Holy Spirit, but to activate the believer in them as well. Nothing can replace the experience of hearing God's voice for yourself and seeing the Holy Spirit bless another through your obedience. The author has had nearly forty years of experience moving in the Holy Spirit and shares the lessons learned through life. He is candid and simple in his approach to this much-needed subject.

Releasing Healing and Signs and Wonders Seminar

This seminar is designed to give practical and biblical guidelines for releasing faith for healing and miracles. This is not just a teaching session, but is a hands-on time of release and activation in the supernatural arena.

The author has witnessed a myriad of healings and miracles done through the ministry of the saints as they responded to the Holy Spirit.

Moving in the Prophetic Seminar

With over nearly forty years of experience in this area, the author is equipped to share practical, biblical truth concerning this much-needed area of ministry. Once again the teachings are designed to stimulate faith and action in the individual. The seminar explores such topics as the differences between being prophetic and being a prophet. How prophets can relate to local leadership and function in local and extra-local ministry. The need for being under authority and other important issues facing prophets.

Ministry Contact Information for Dennis De Grasse

Dennis De Grasse
5829 Liner Creek Road
Clyde, NC 28721

Telephone: 828-627-3661

E-mail: ddegrasse@gmail.com

Additional copies of this book and other
book titles from DESTINY IMAGE are
available at your local bookstore.

Call toll-free: 1-800-722-6774.

Send a request for a catalog to:

Destiny Image® Publishers, Inc.
P.O. Box 310
Shippensburg, PA 17257-0310

*"Speaking to the Purposes of God for This
Generation and for the Generations to Come."*

**For a complete list of our titles,
visit us at www.destinyimage.com.**